RABBIT

Coloring Book for Adults

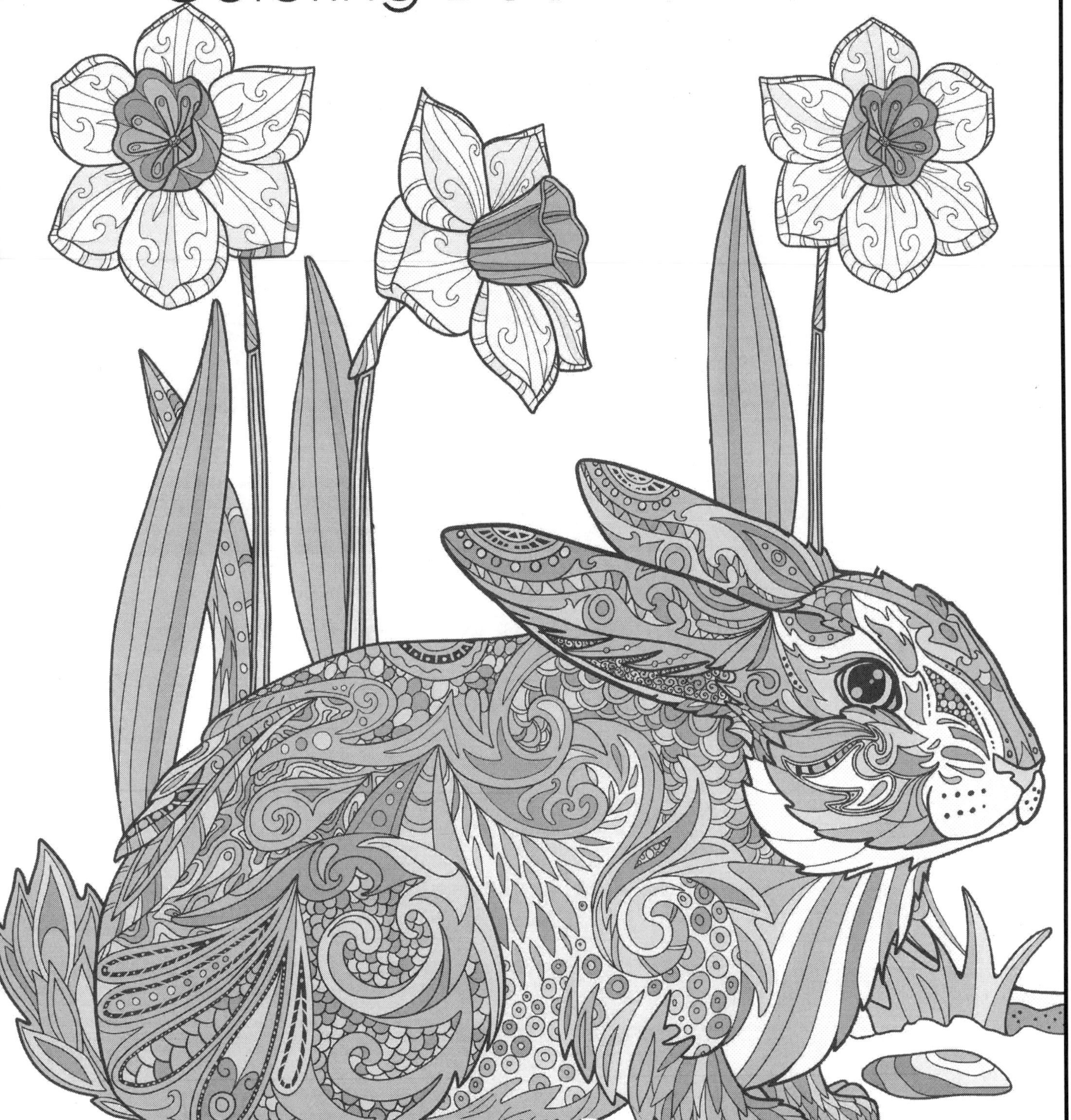

Dylan

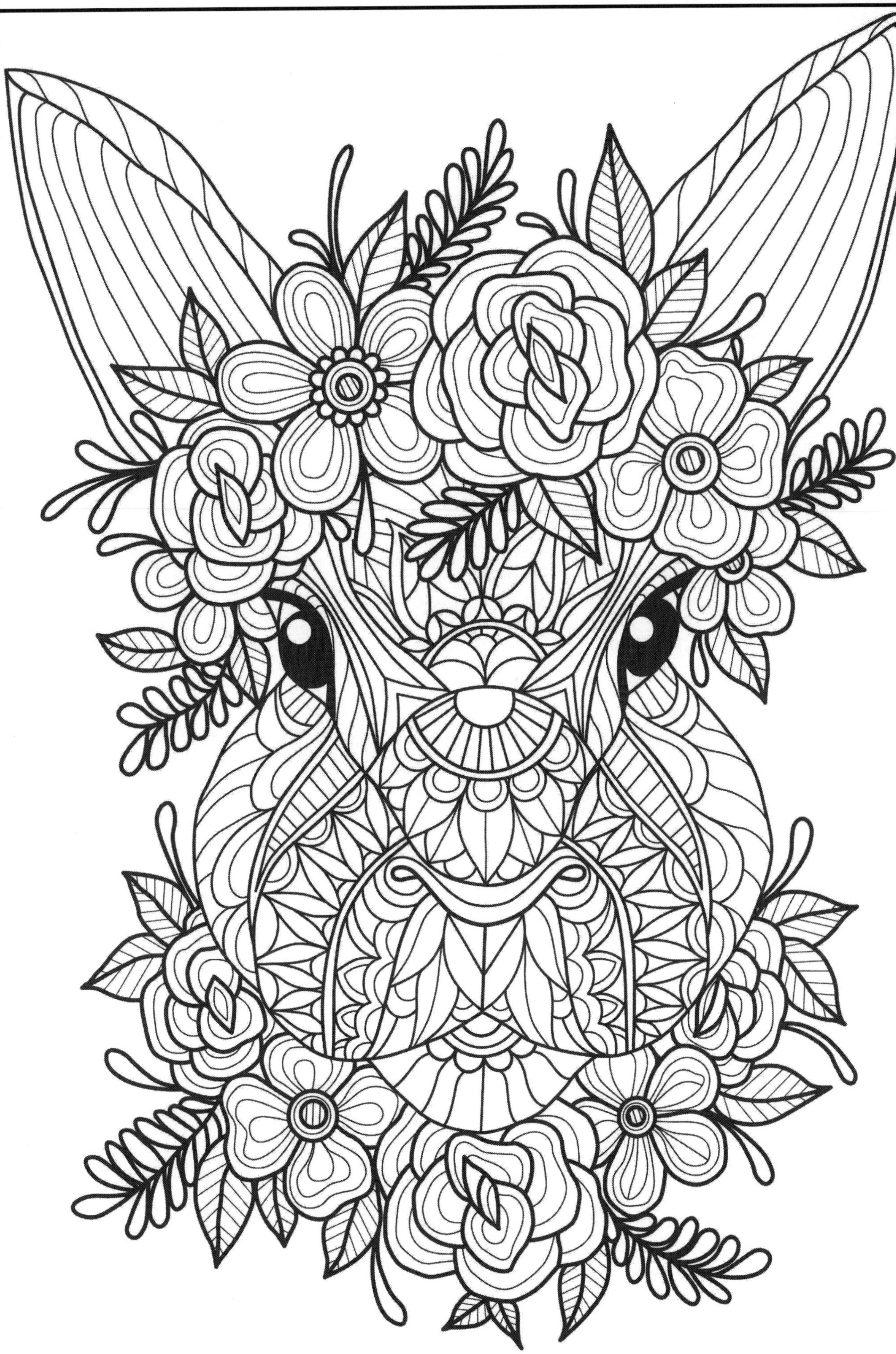

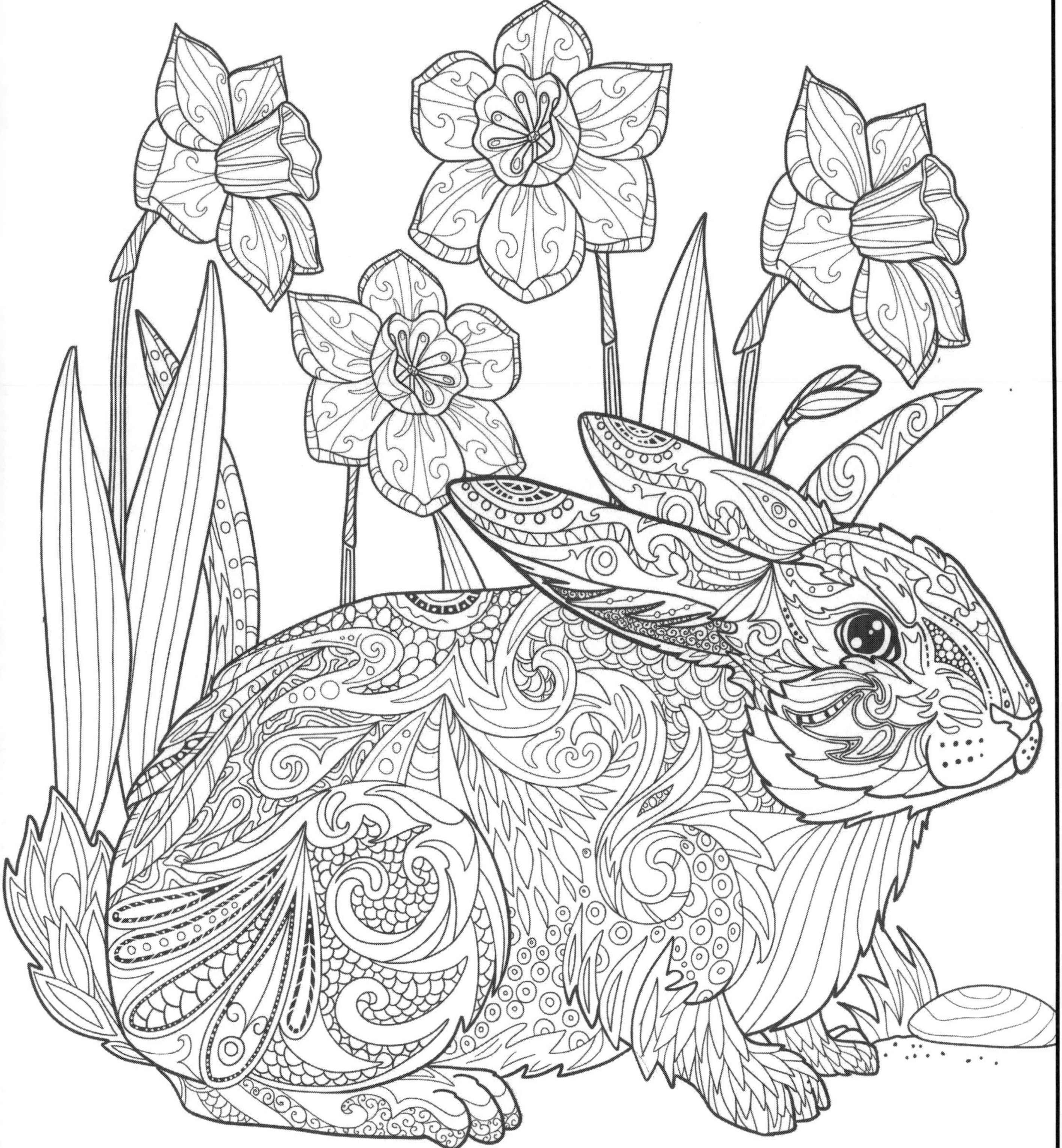

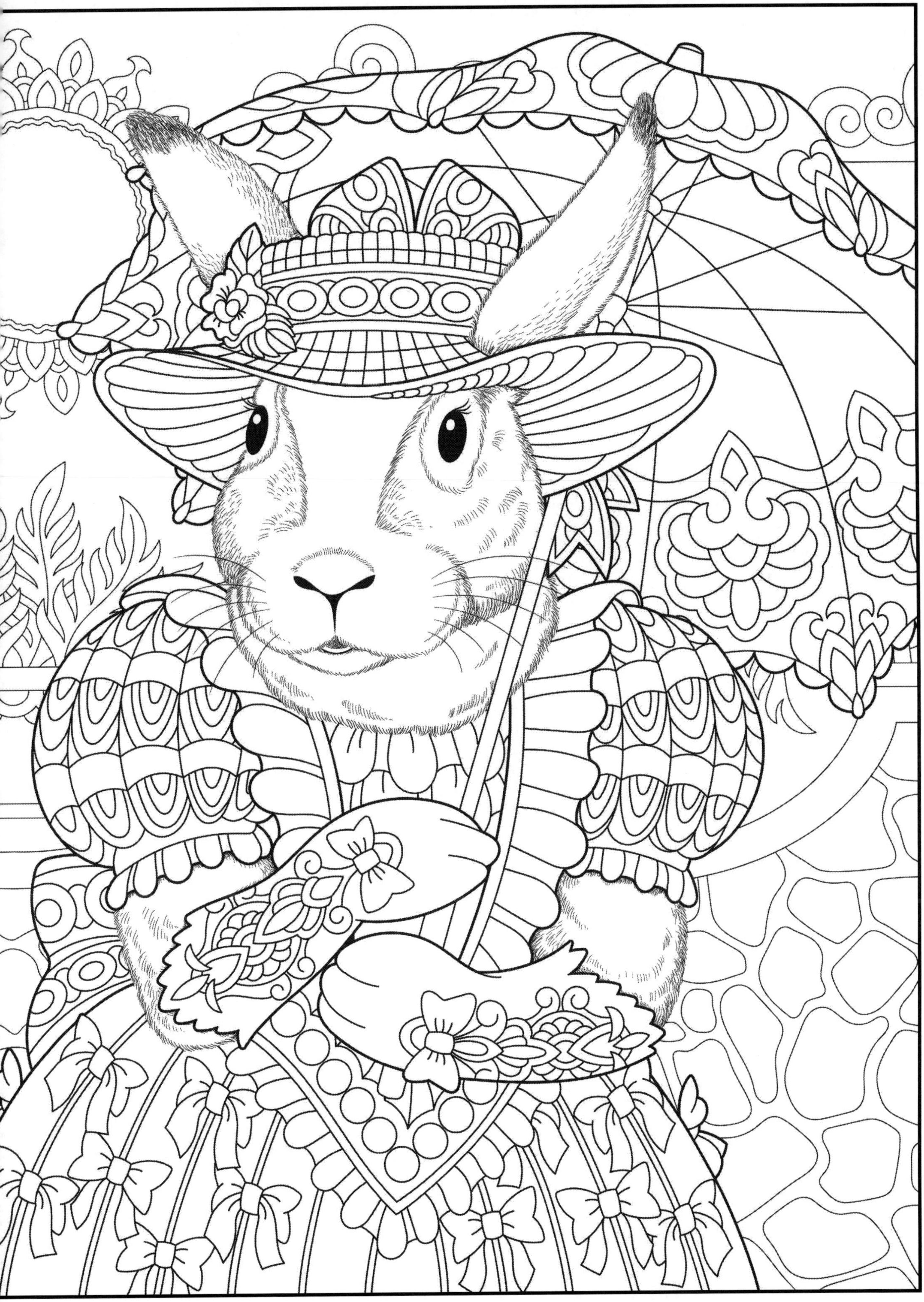

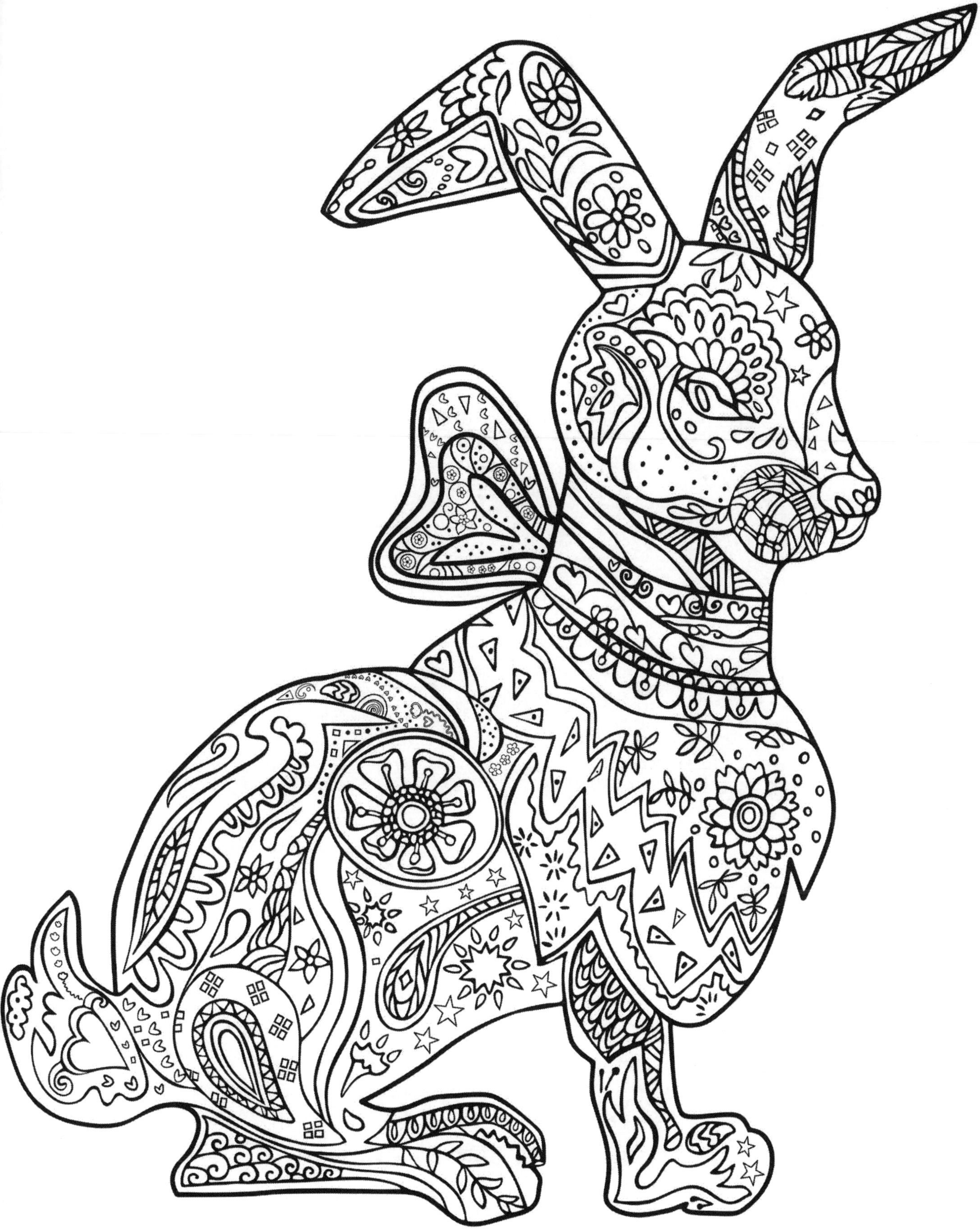

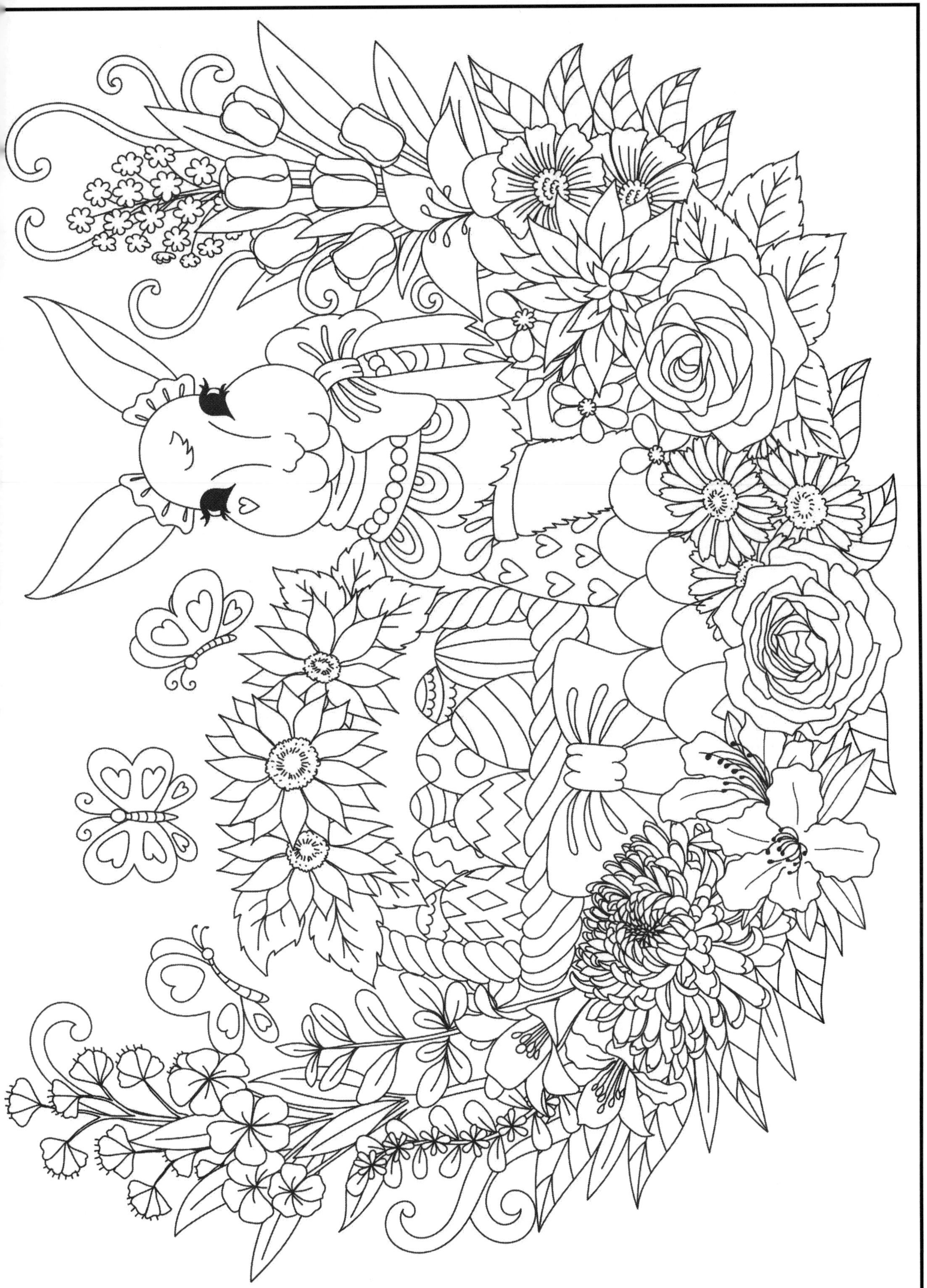

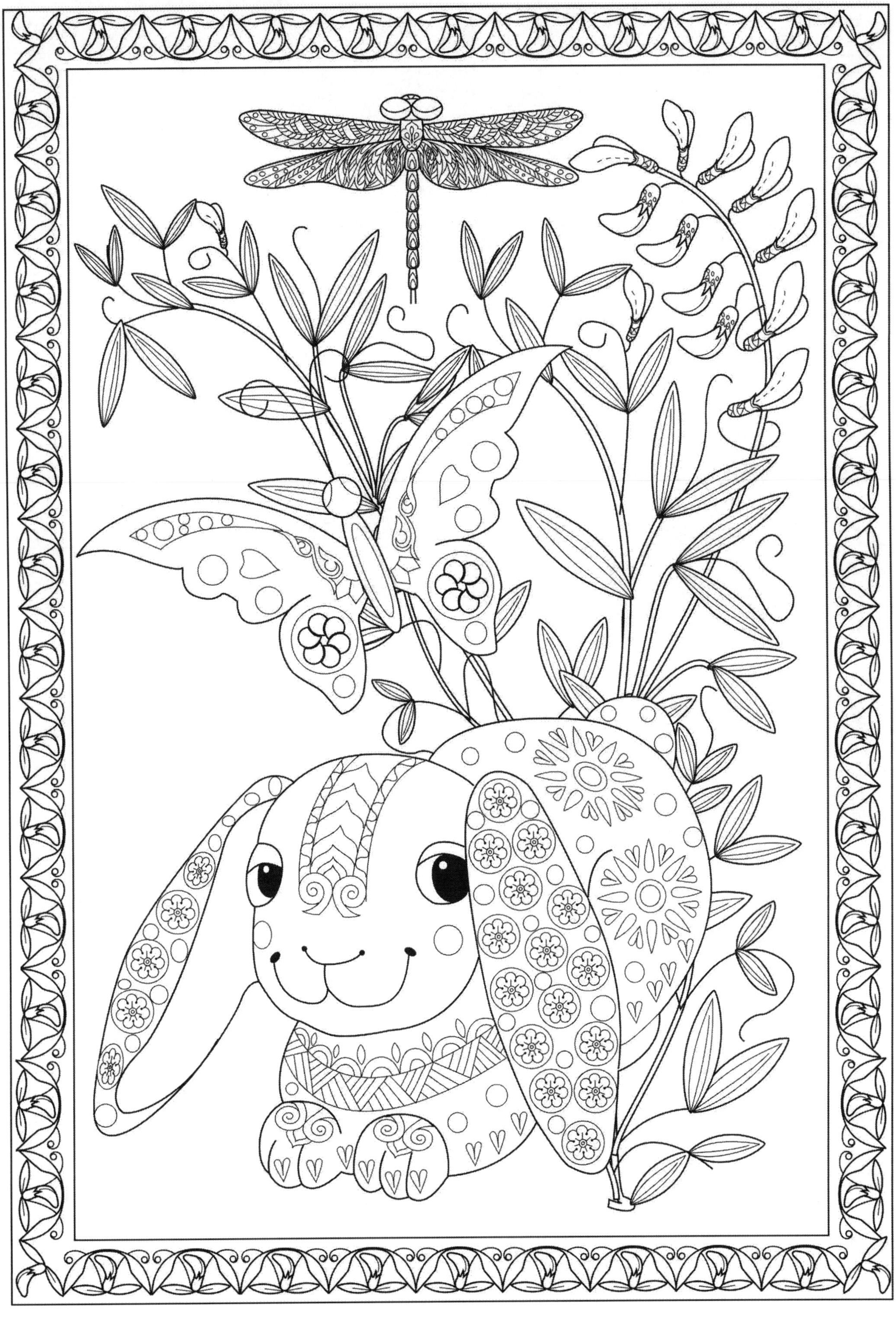

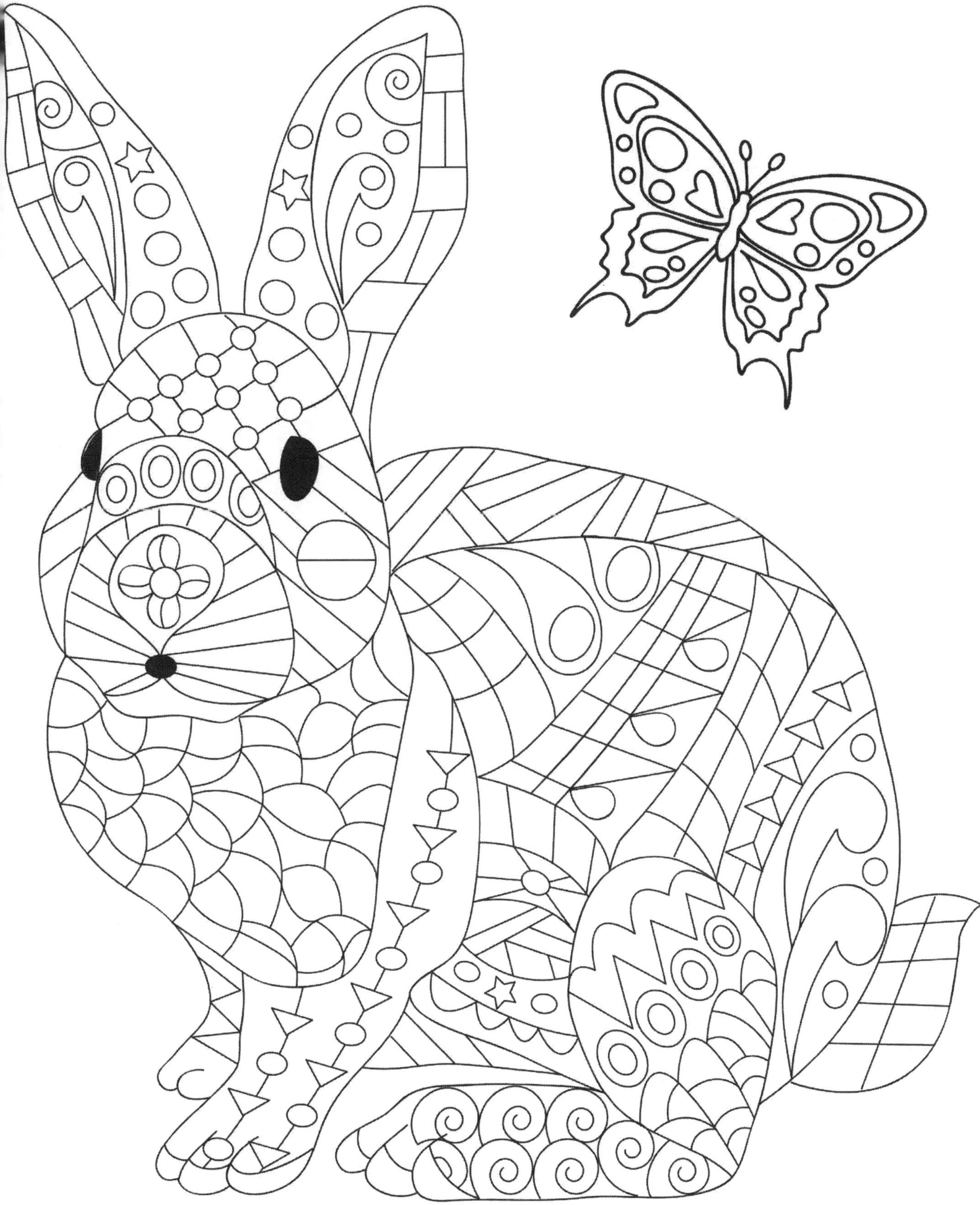

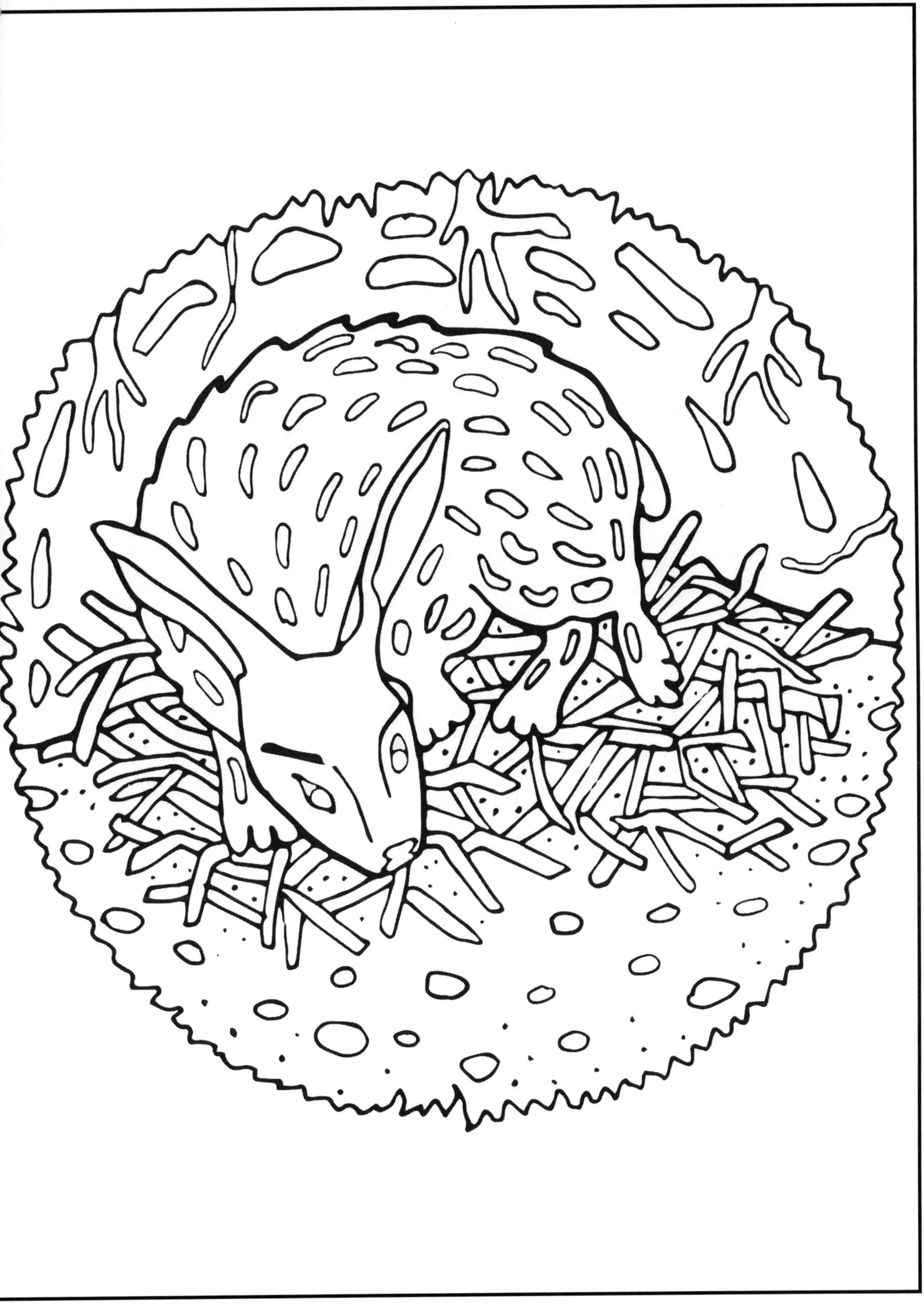

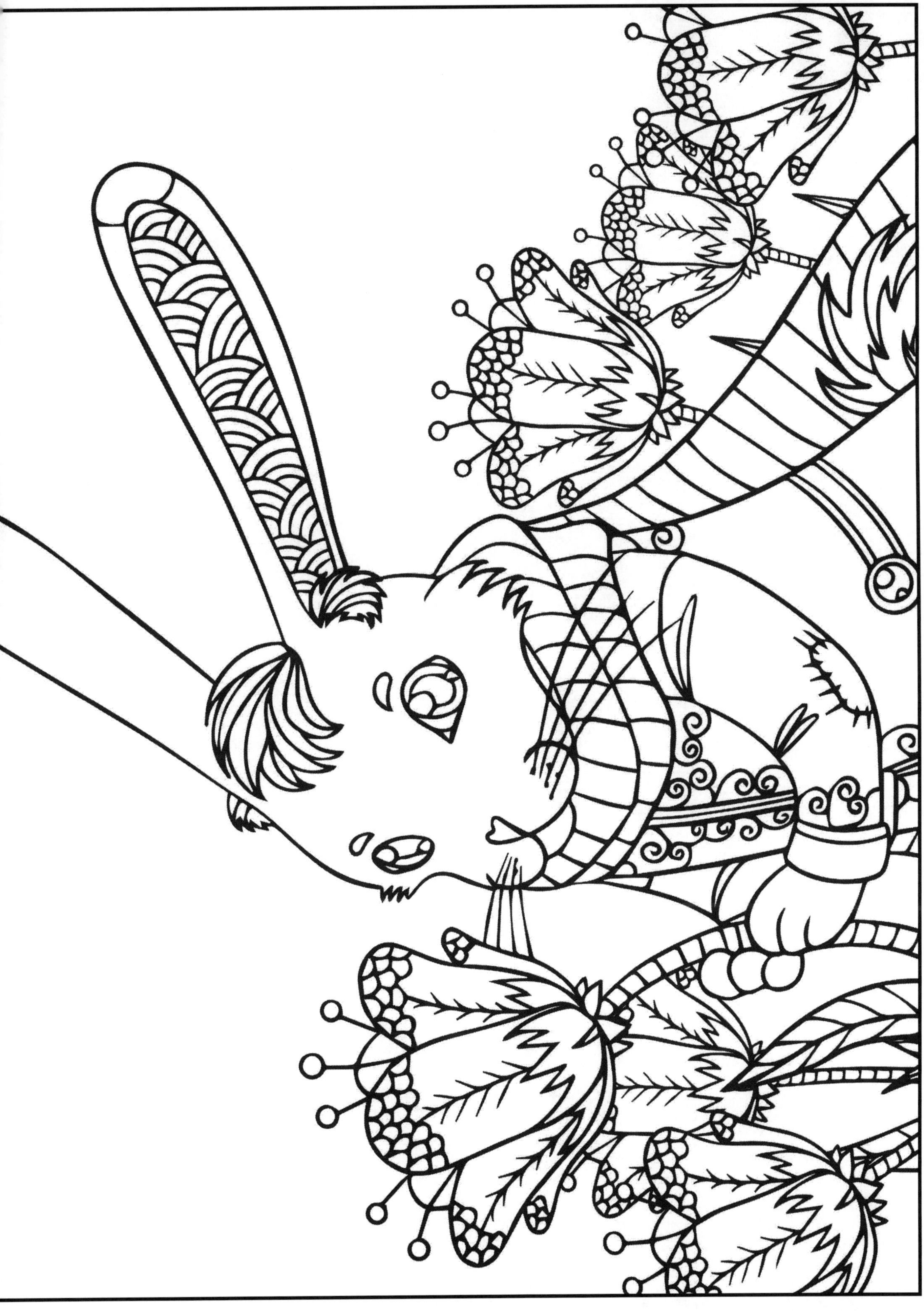

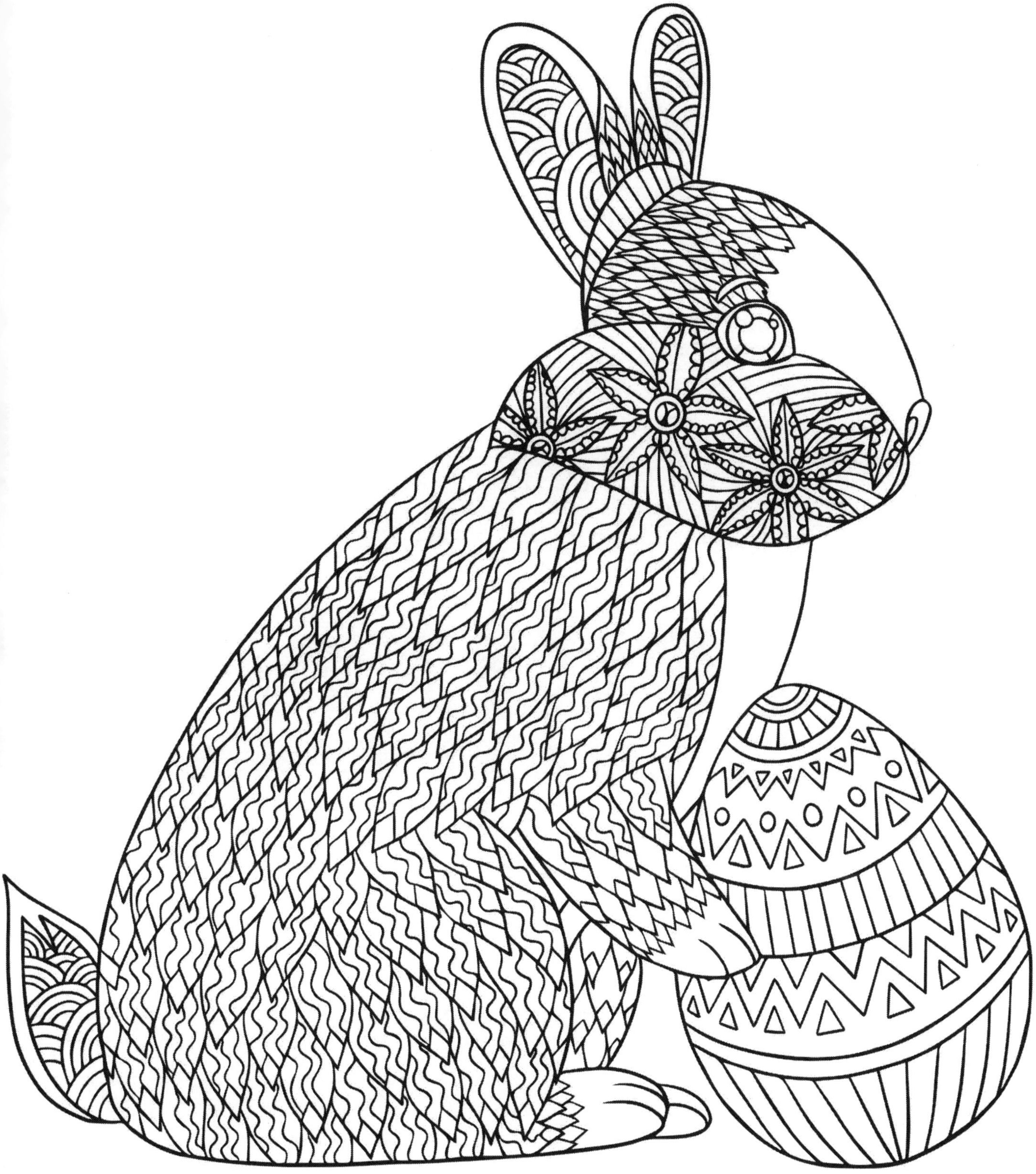

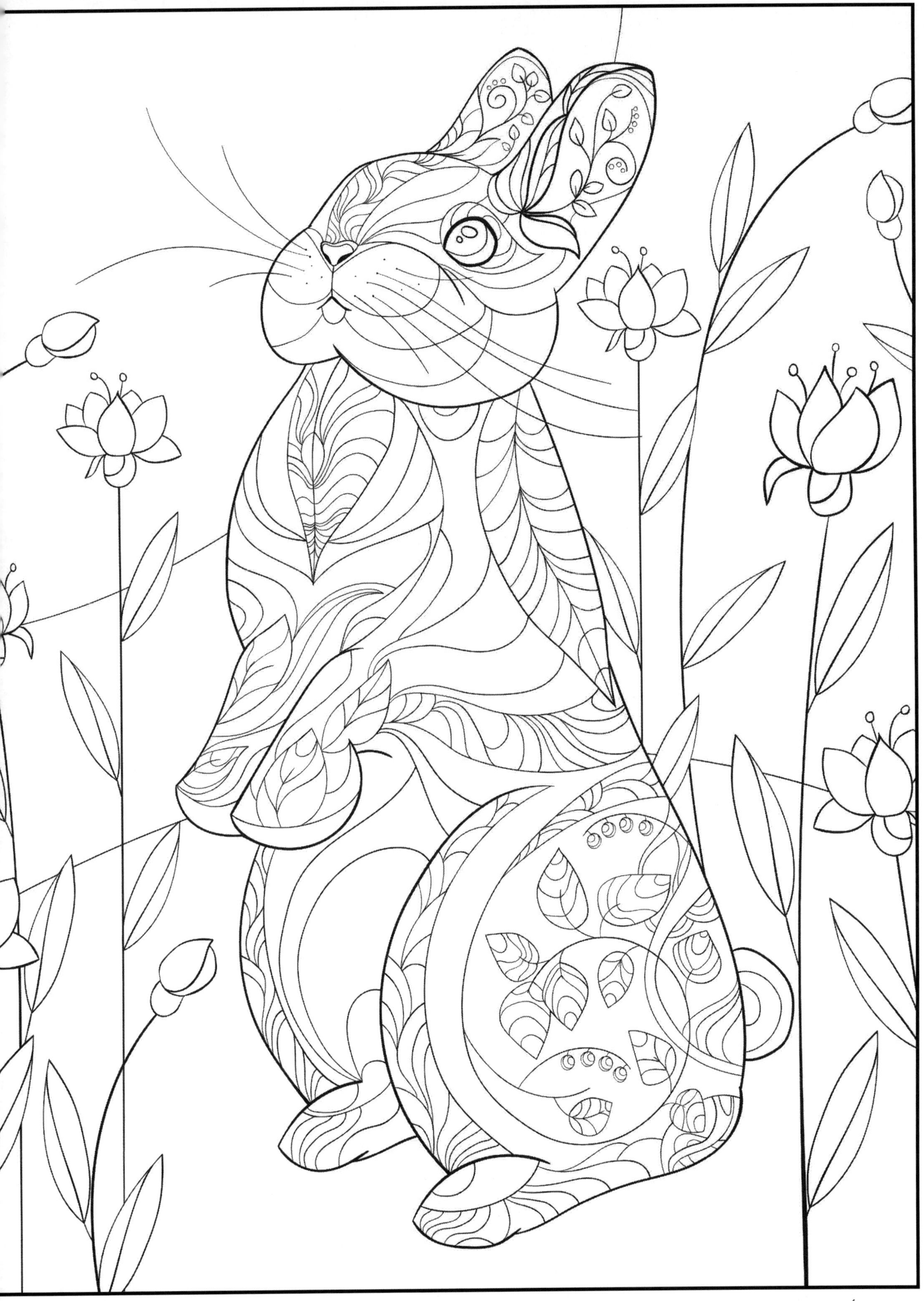

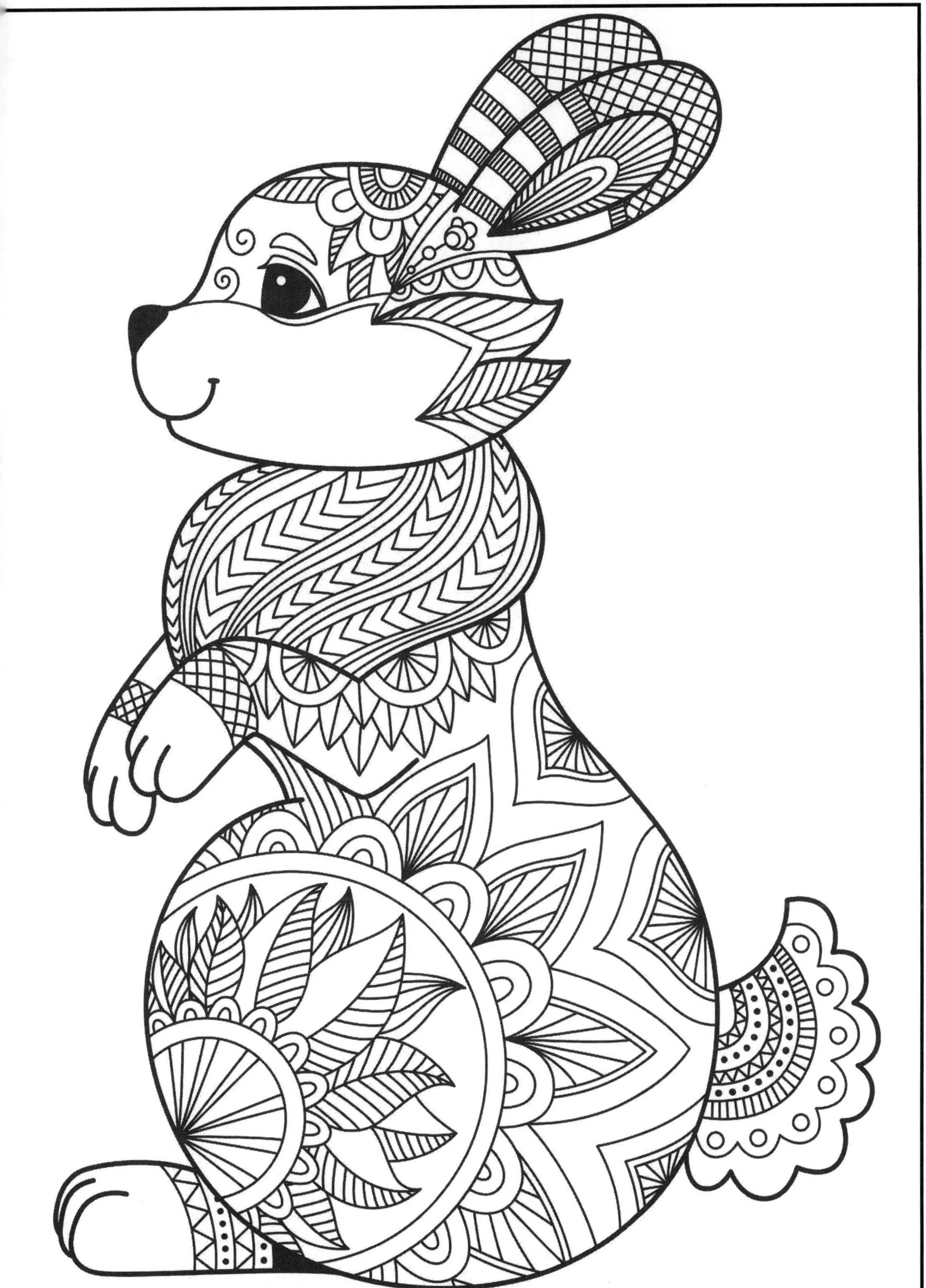

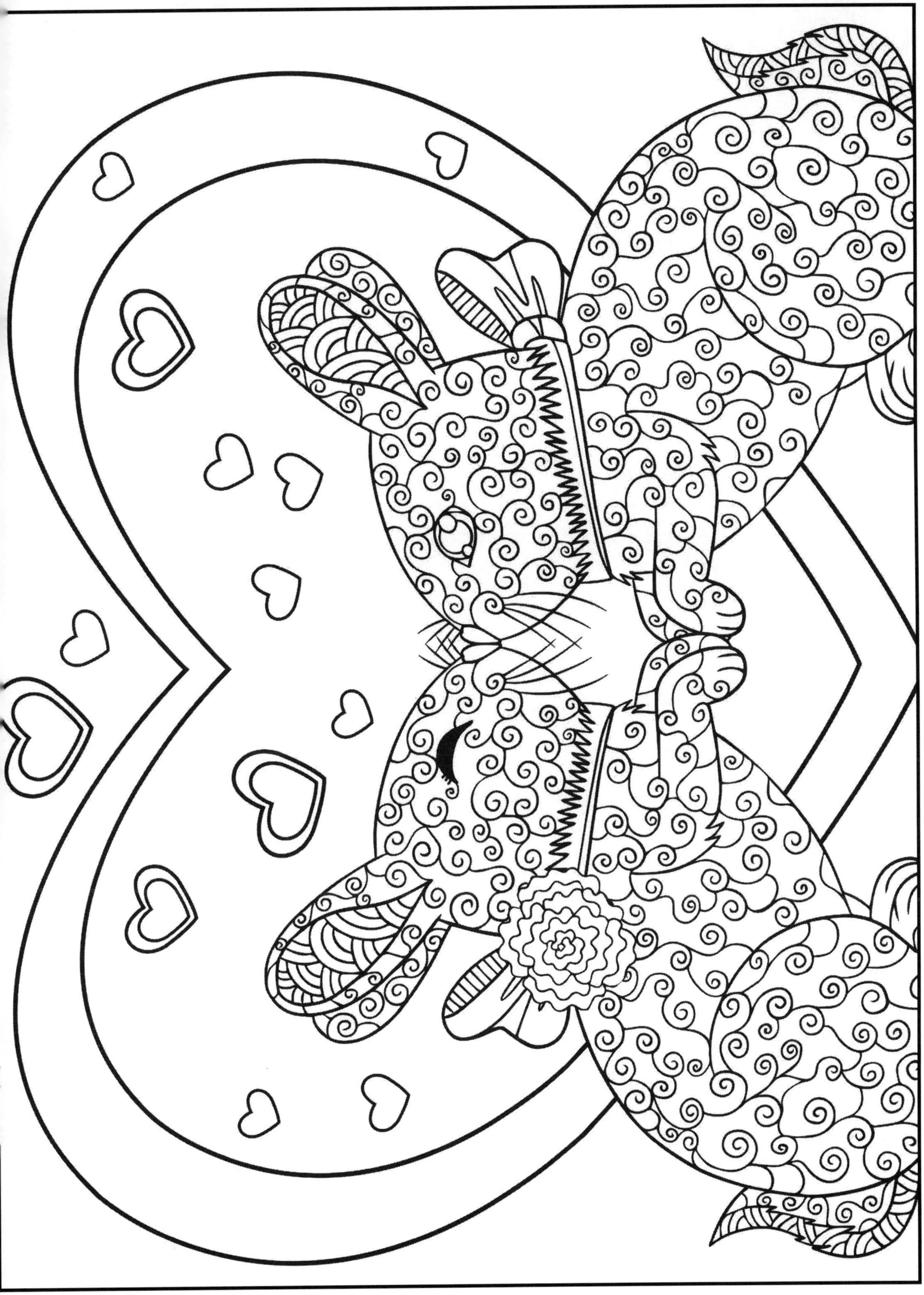

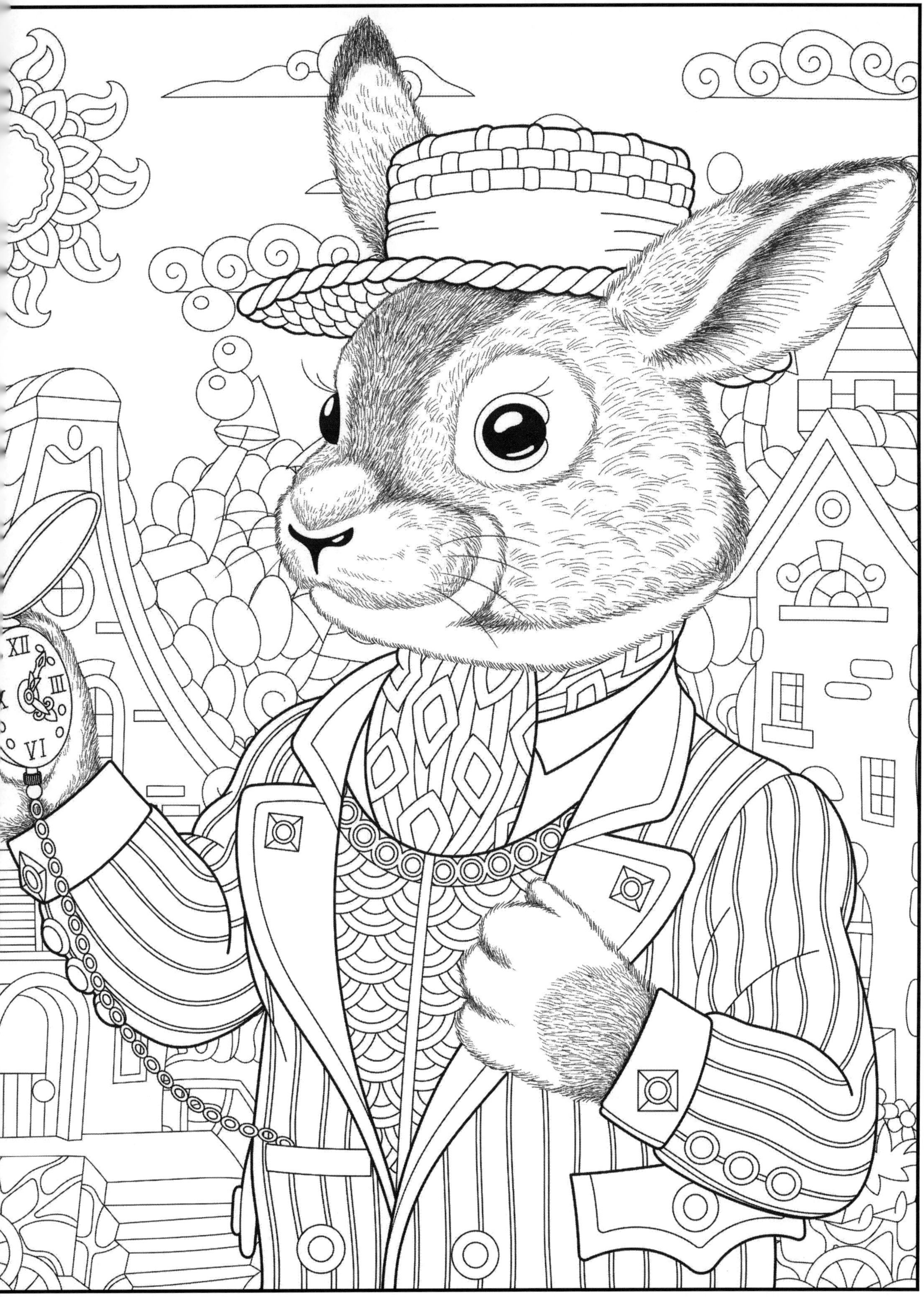
XII
III
VI

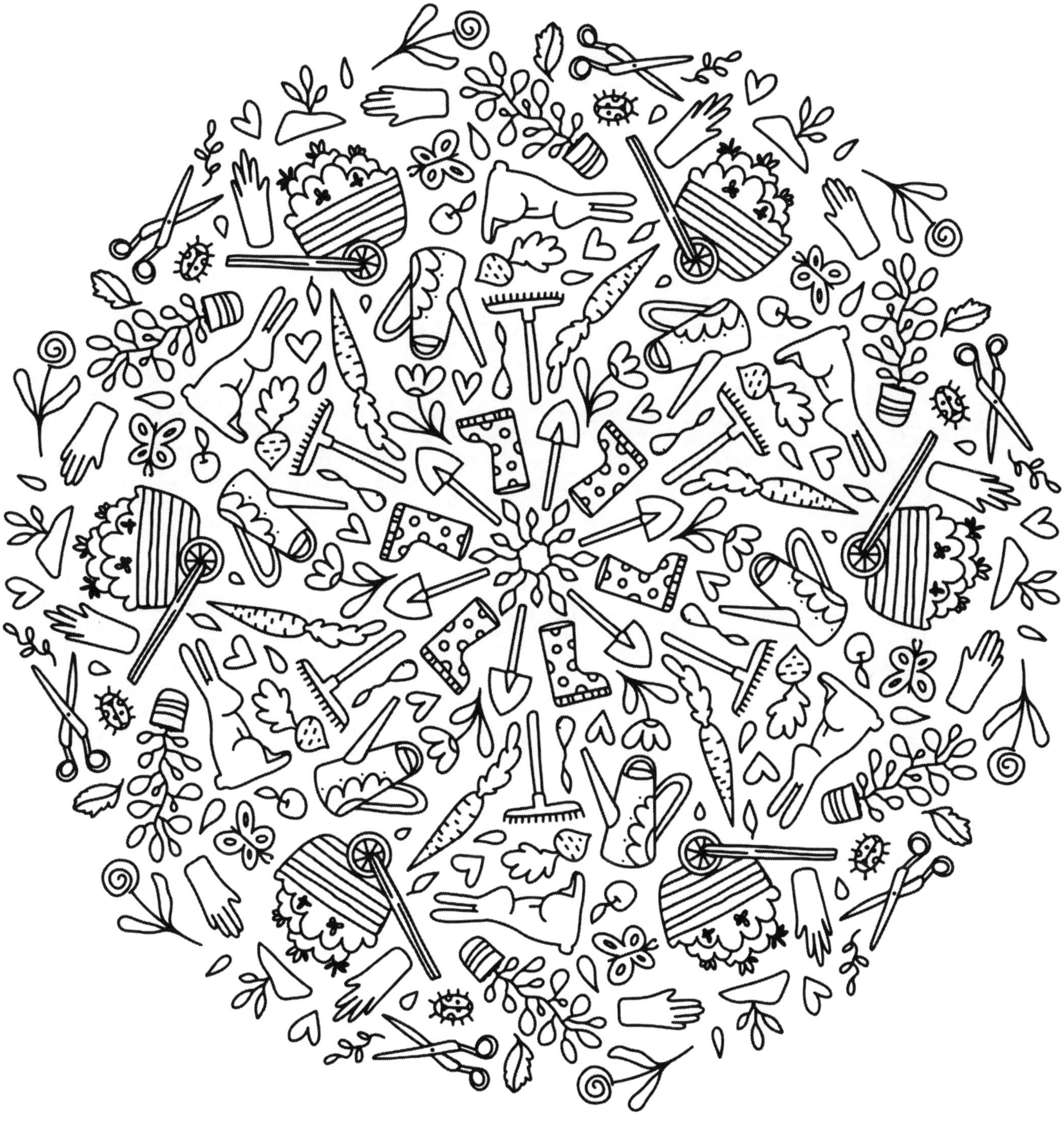

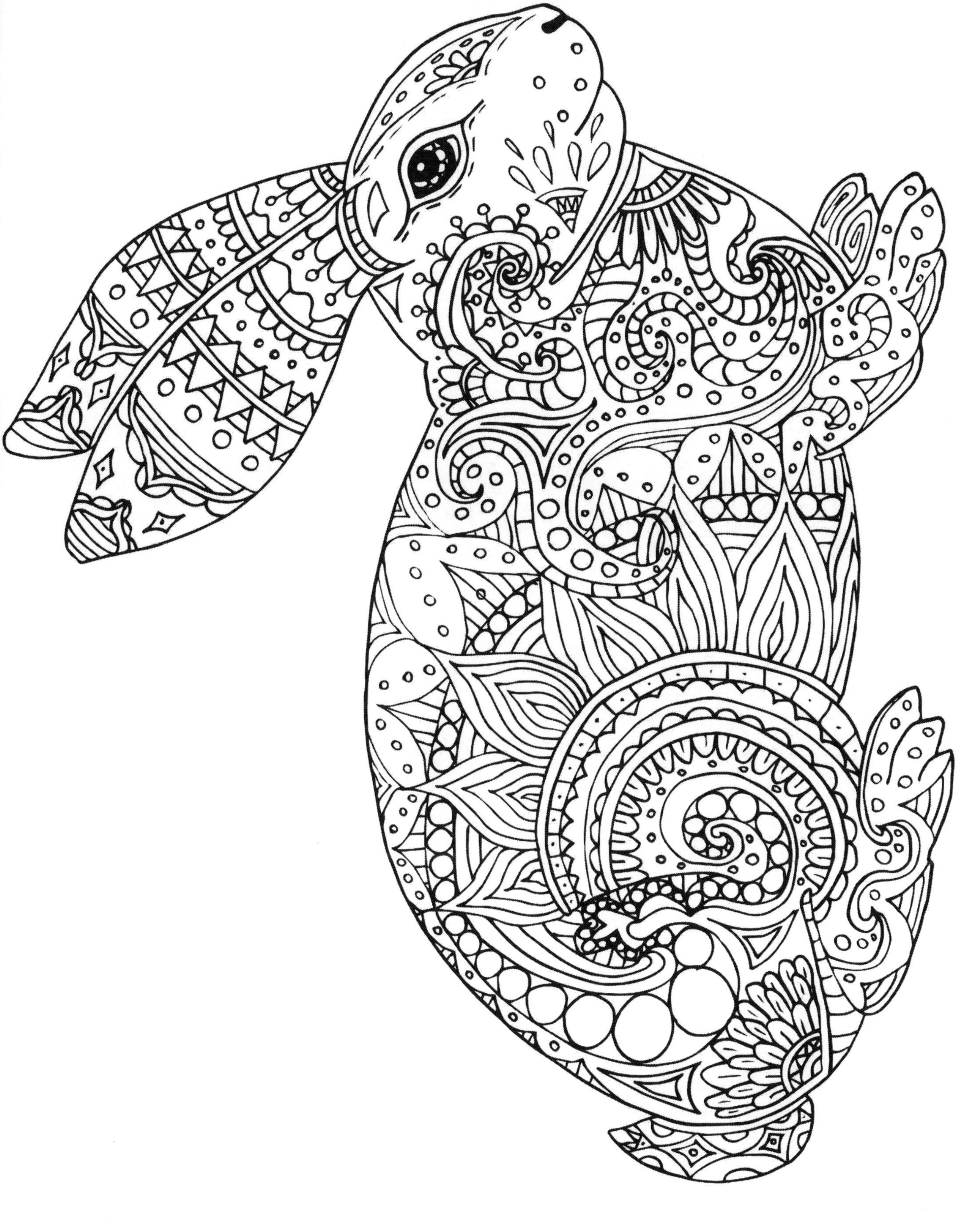

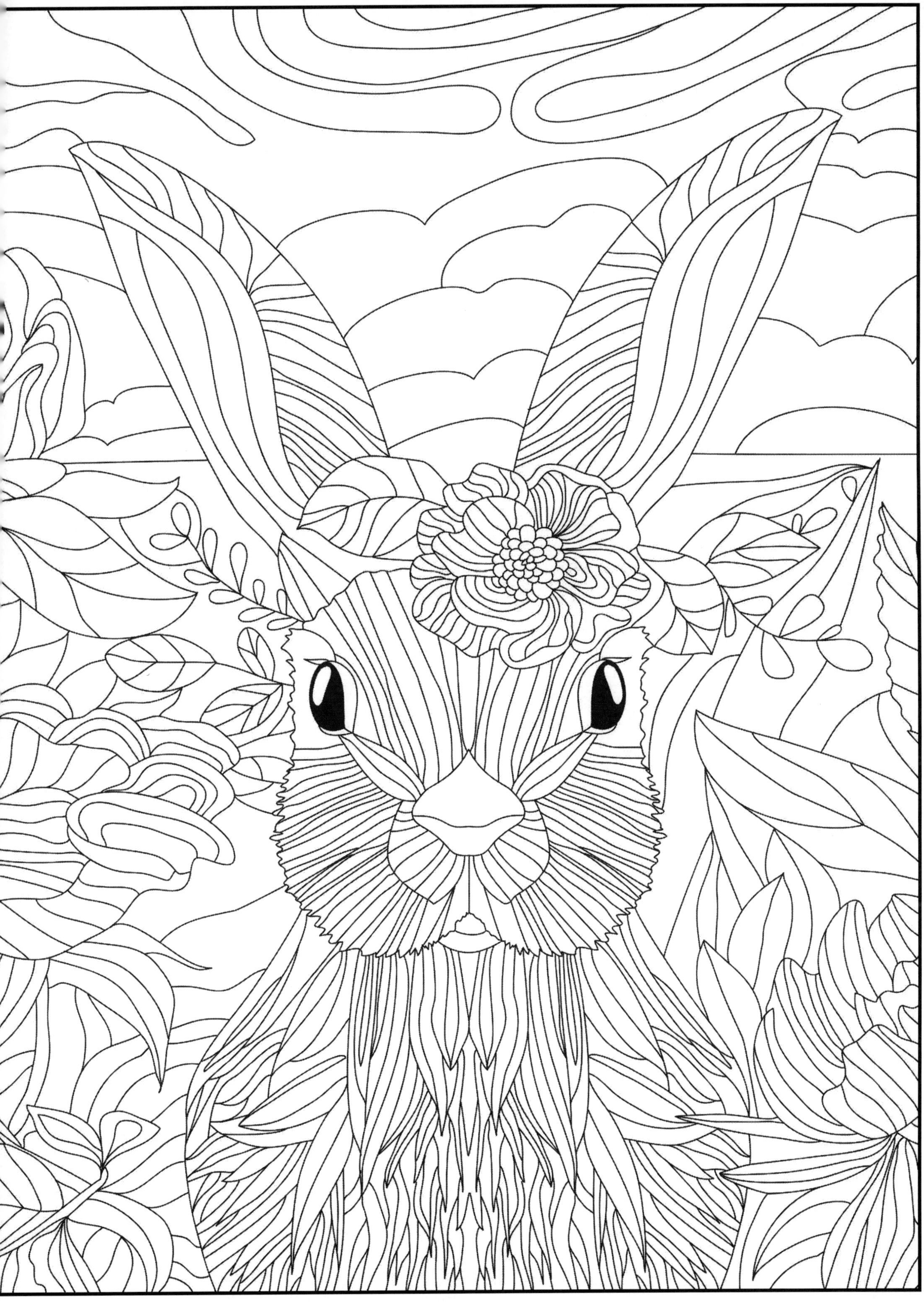

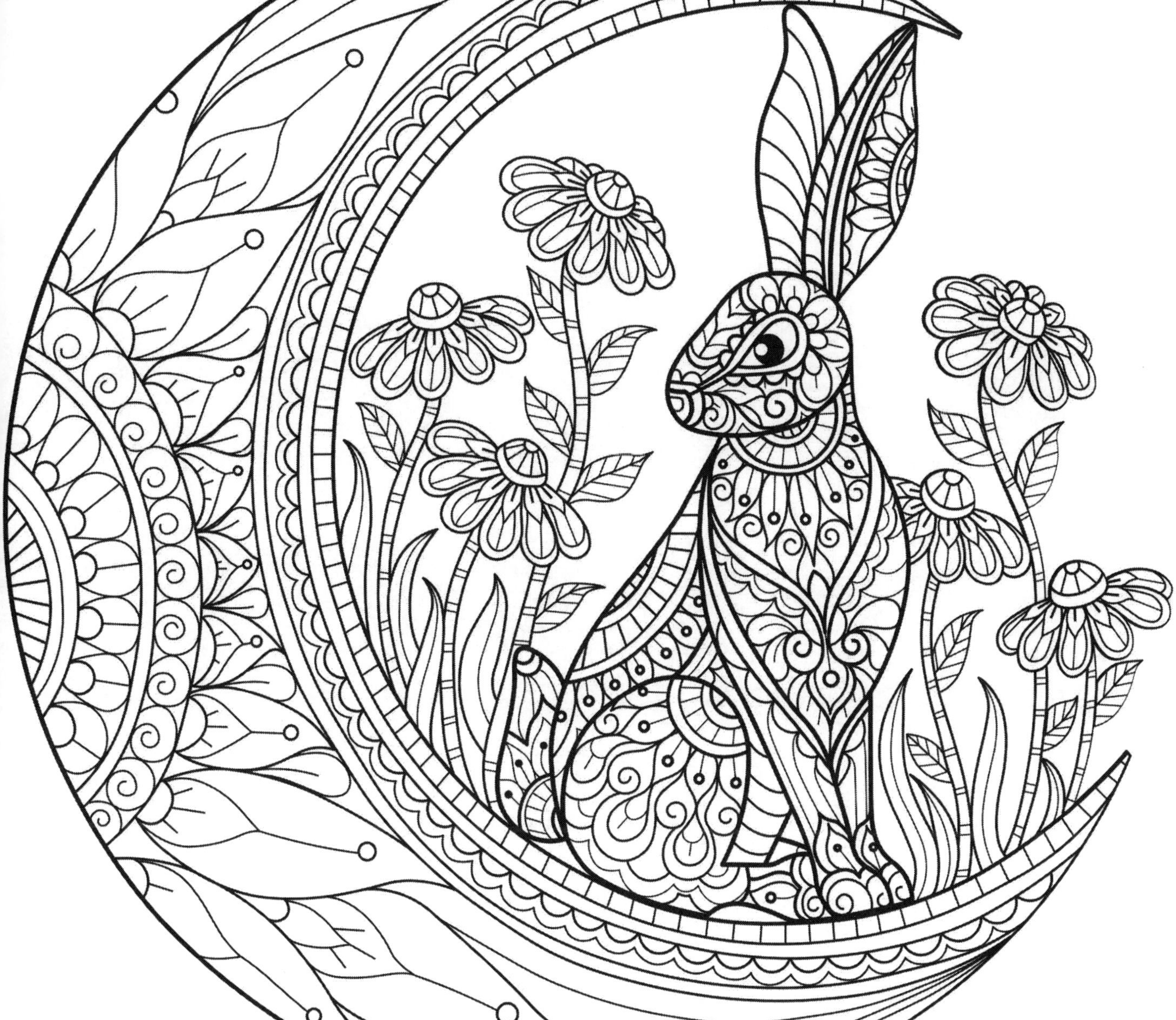

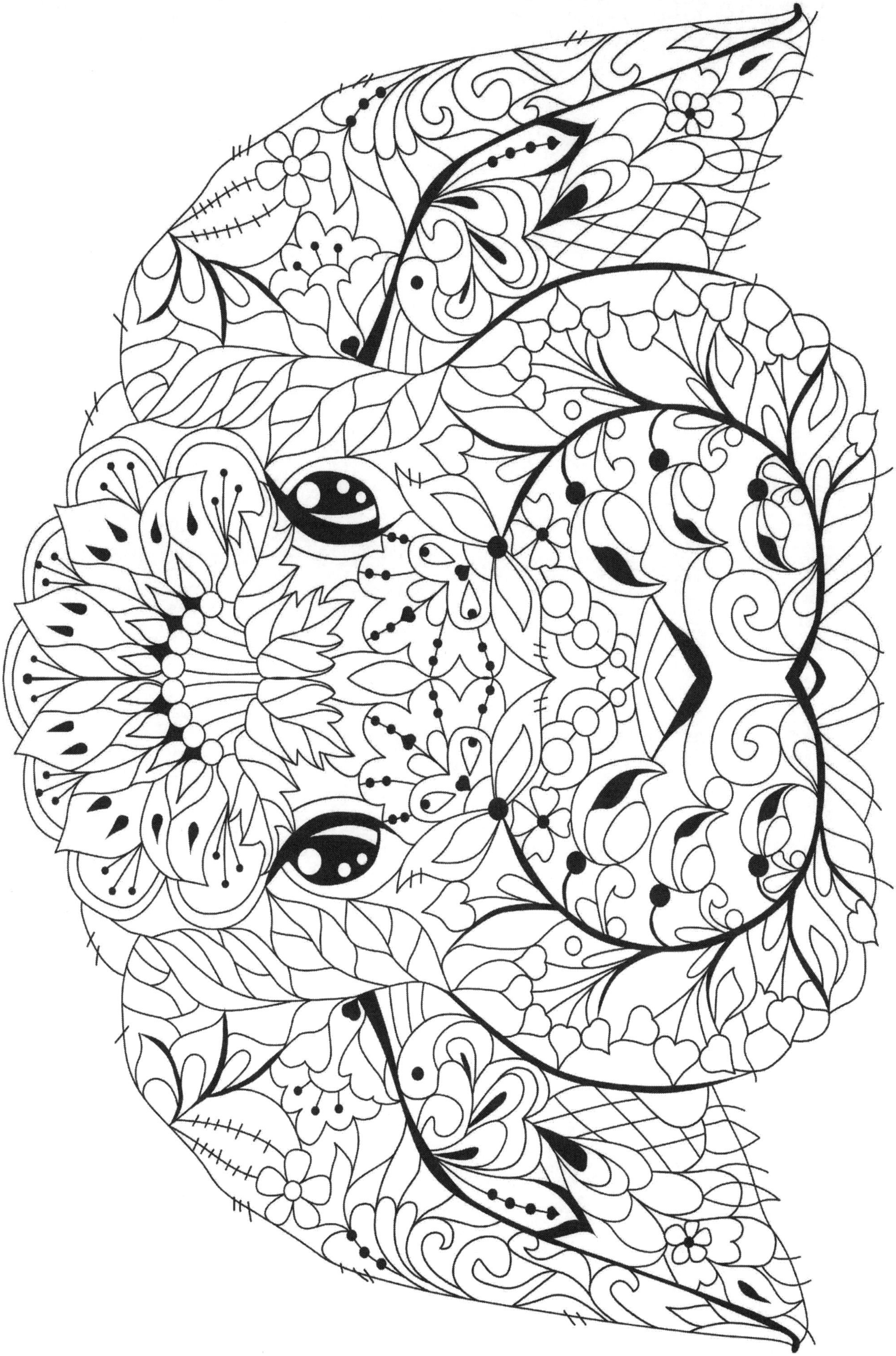

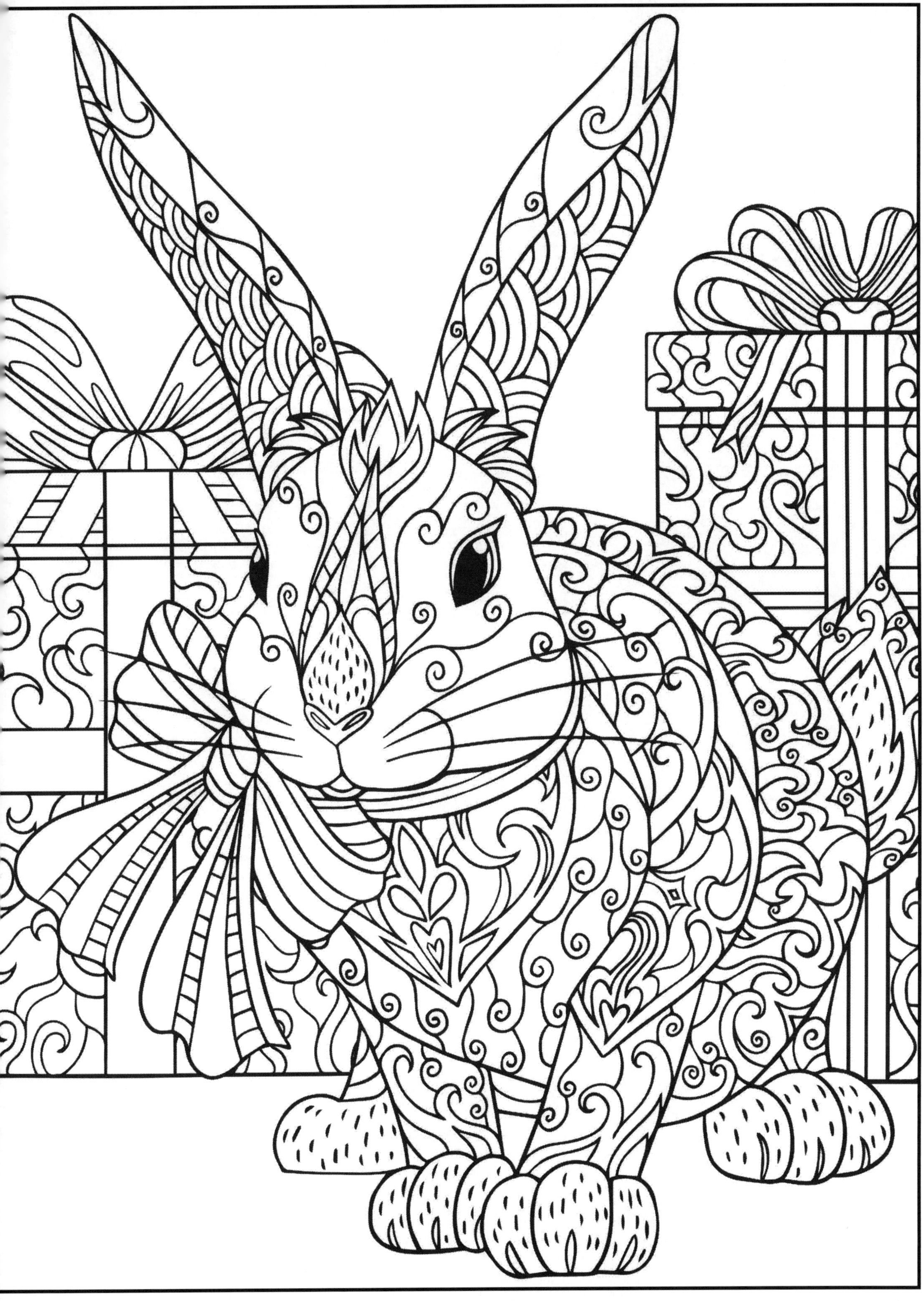

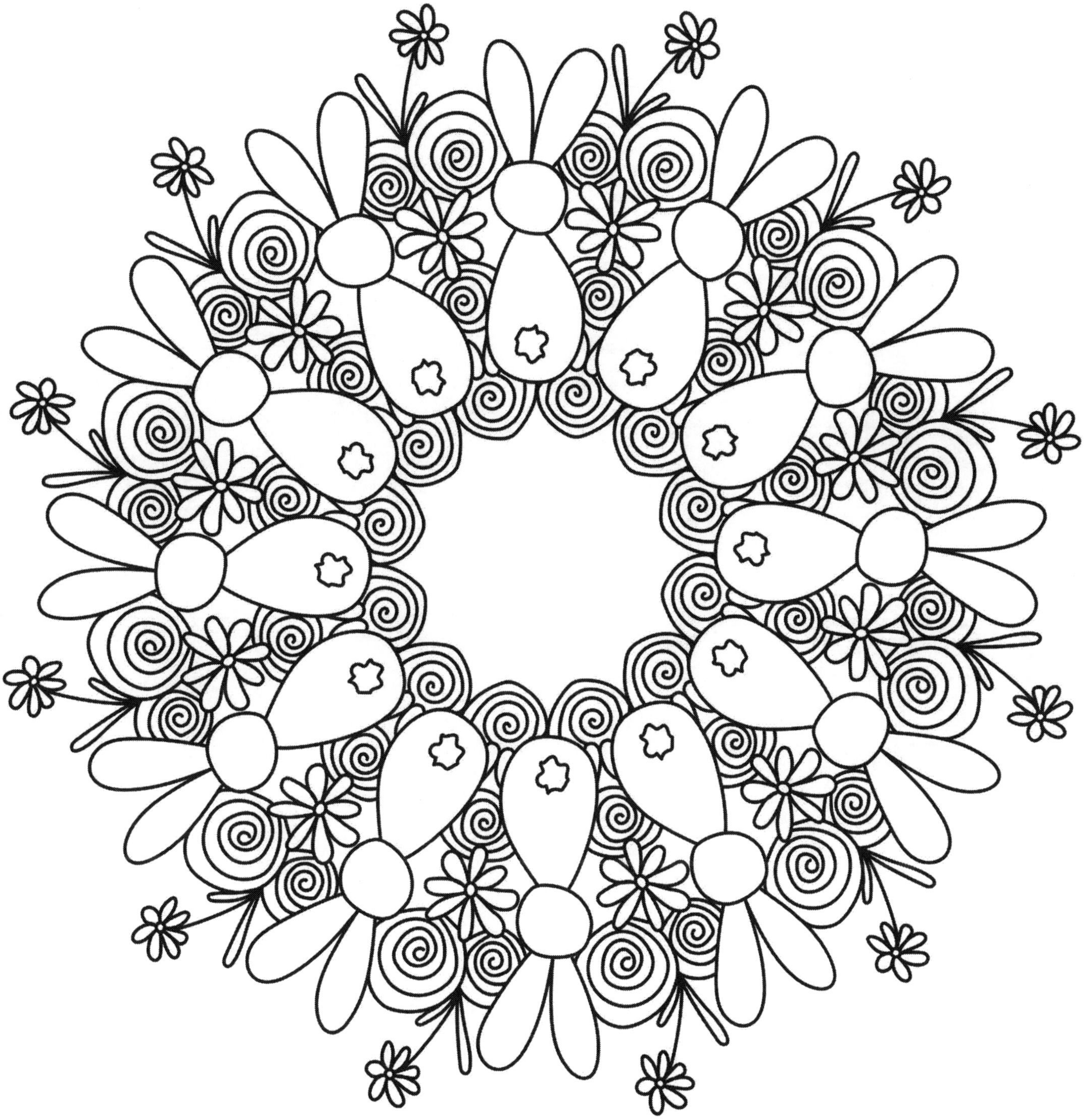

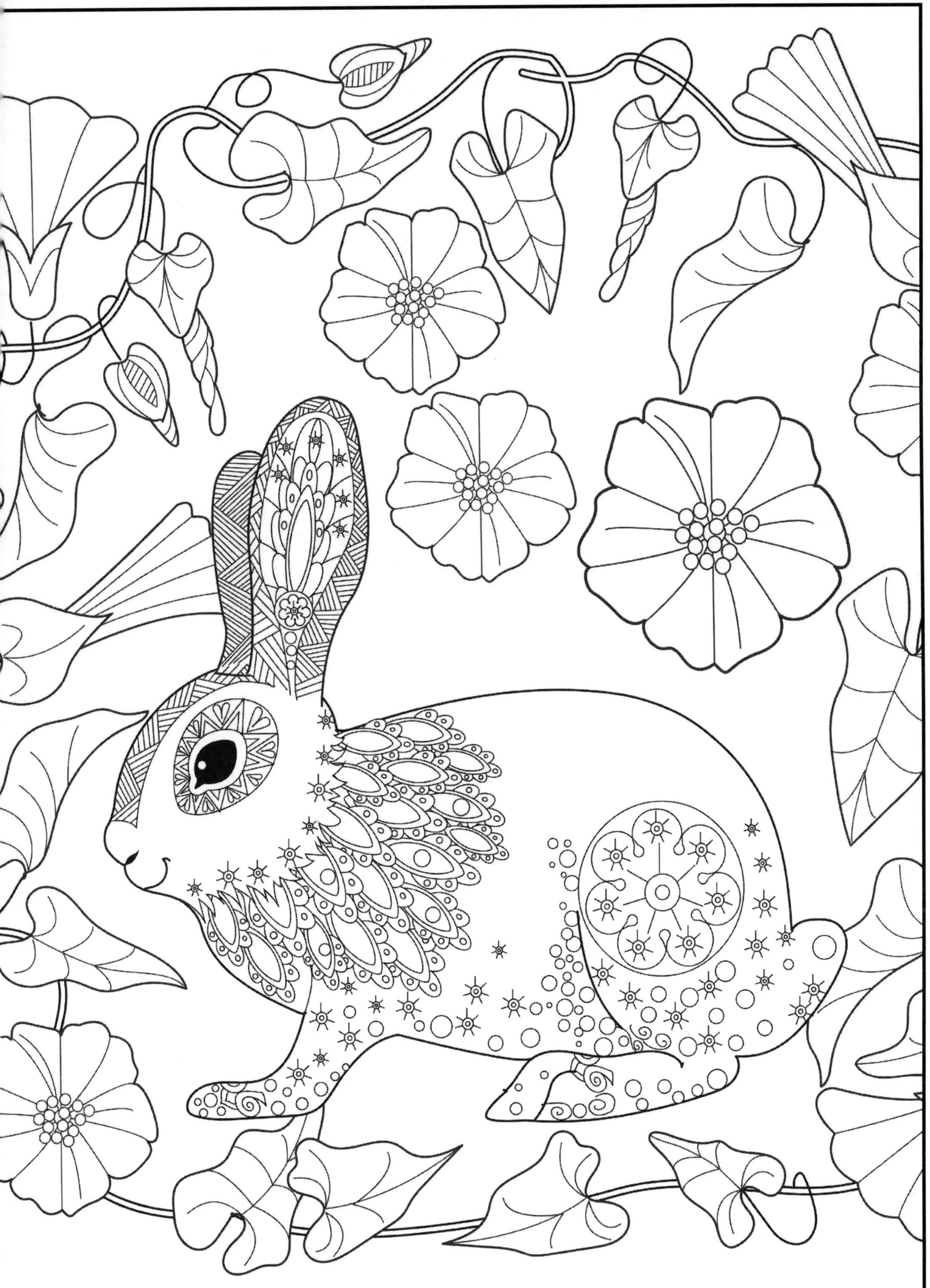

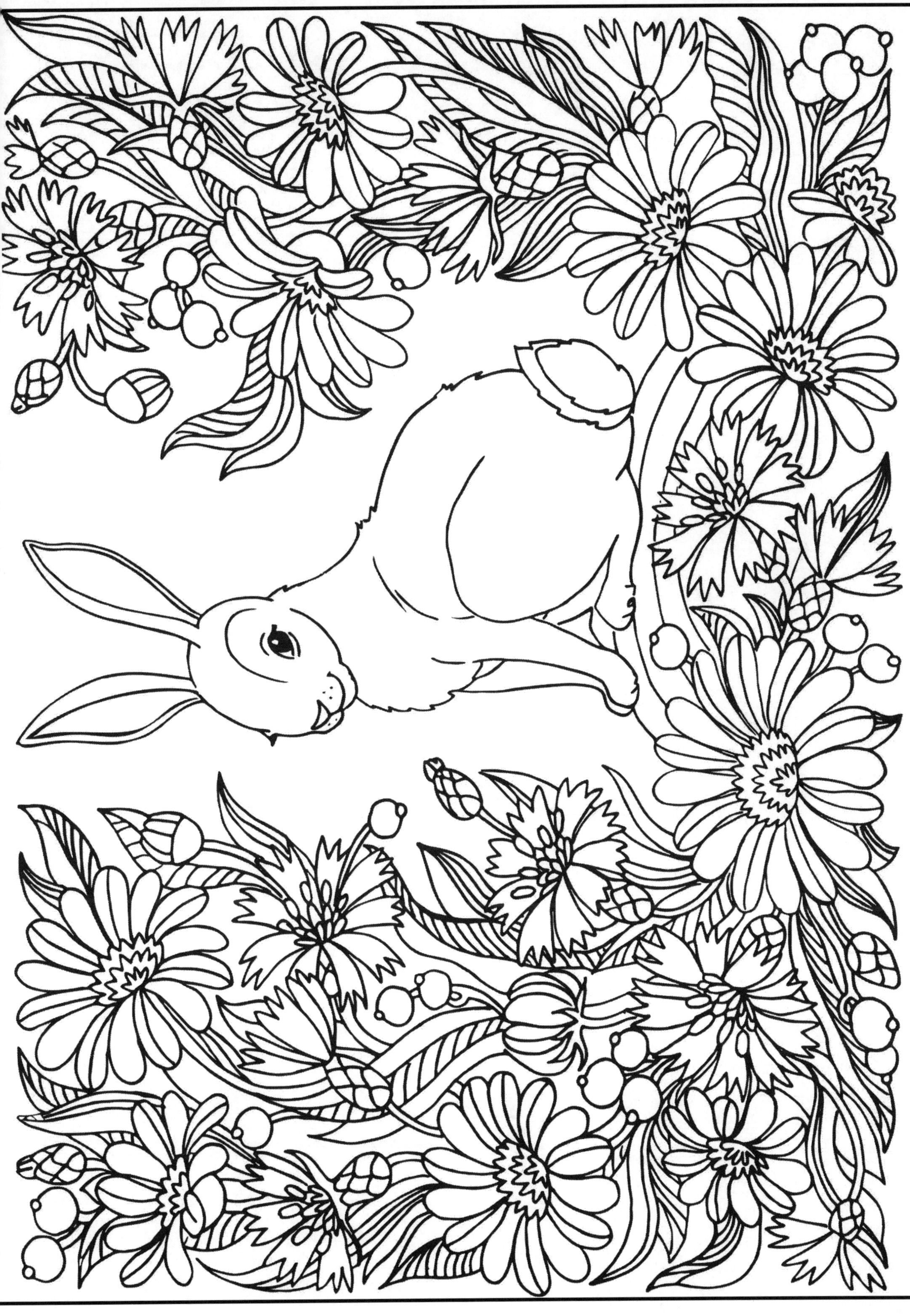

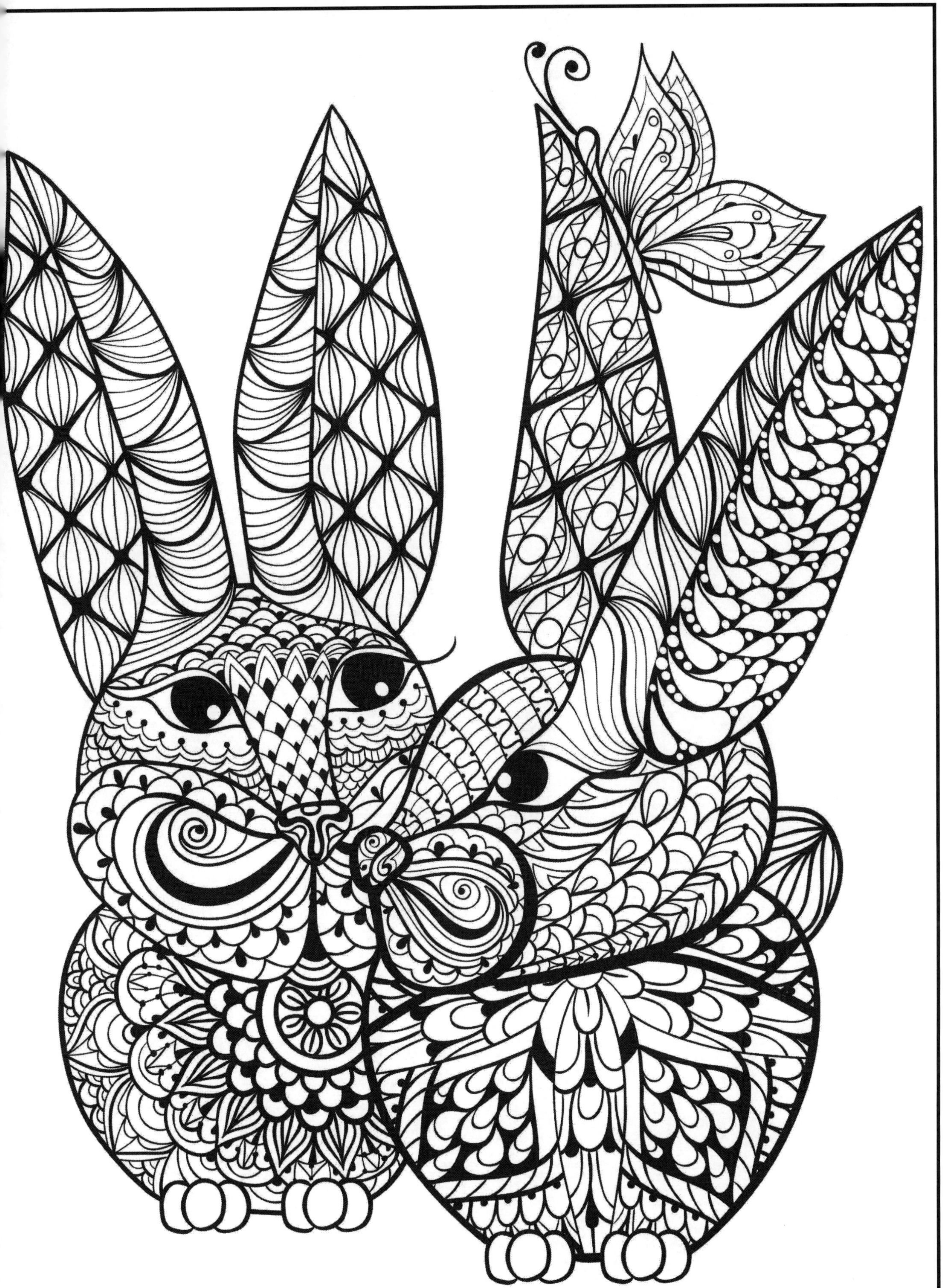

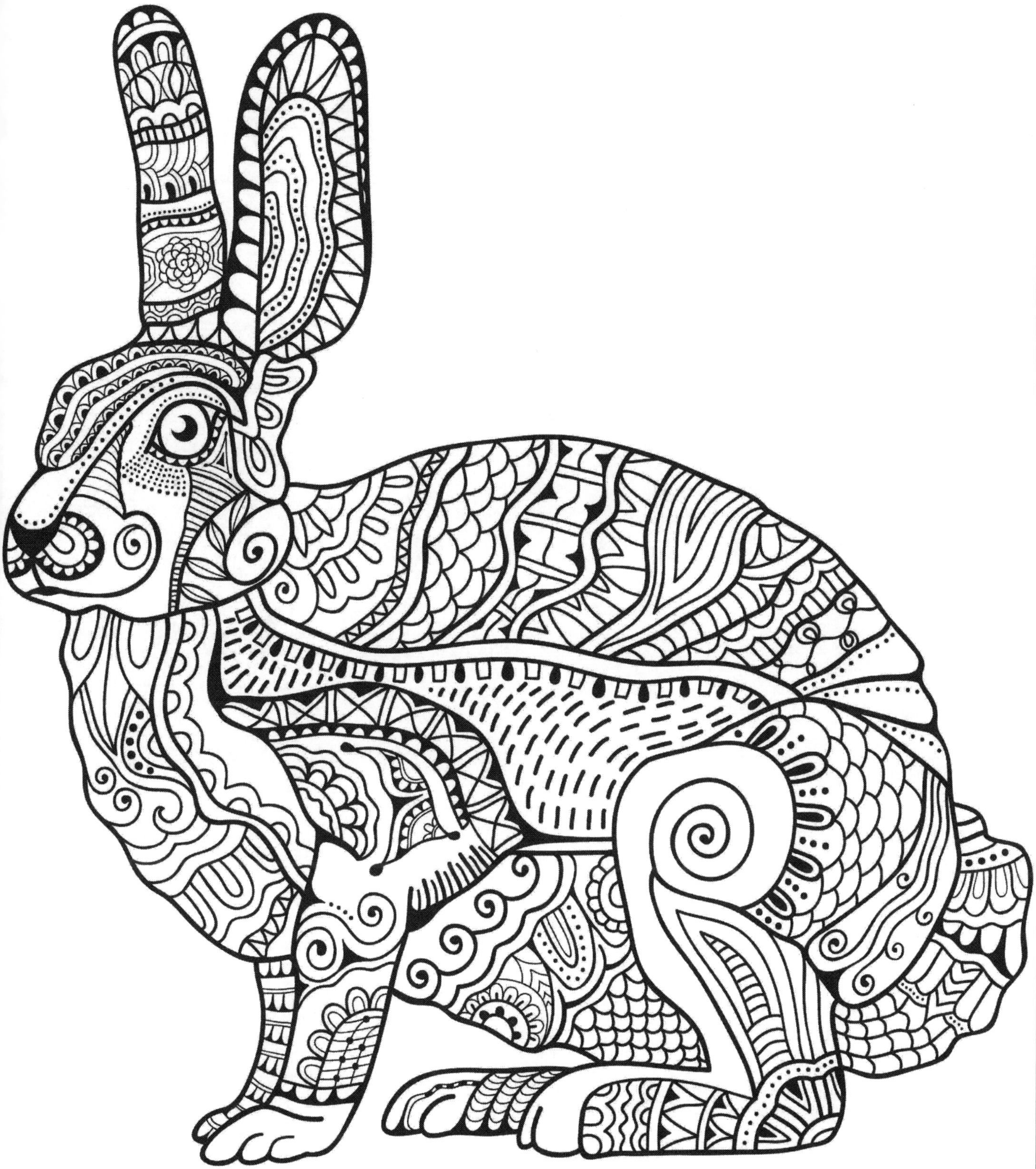

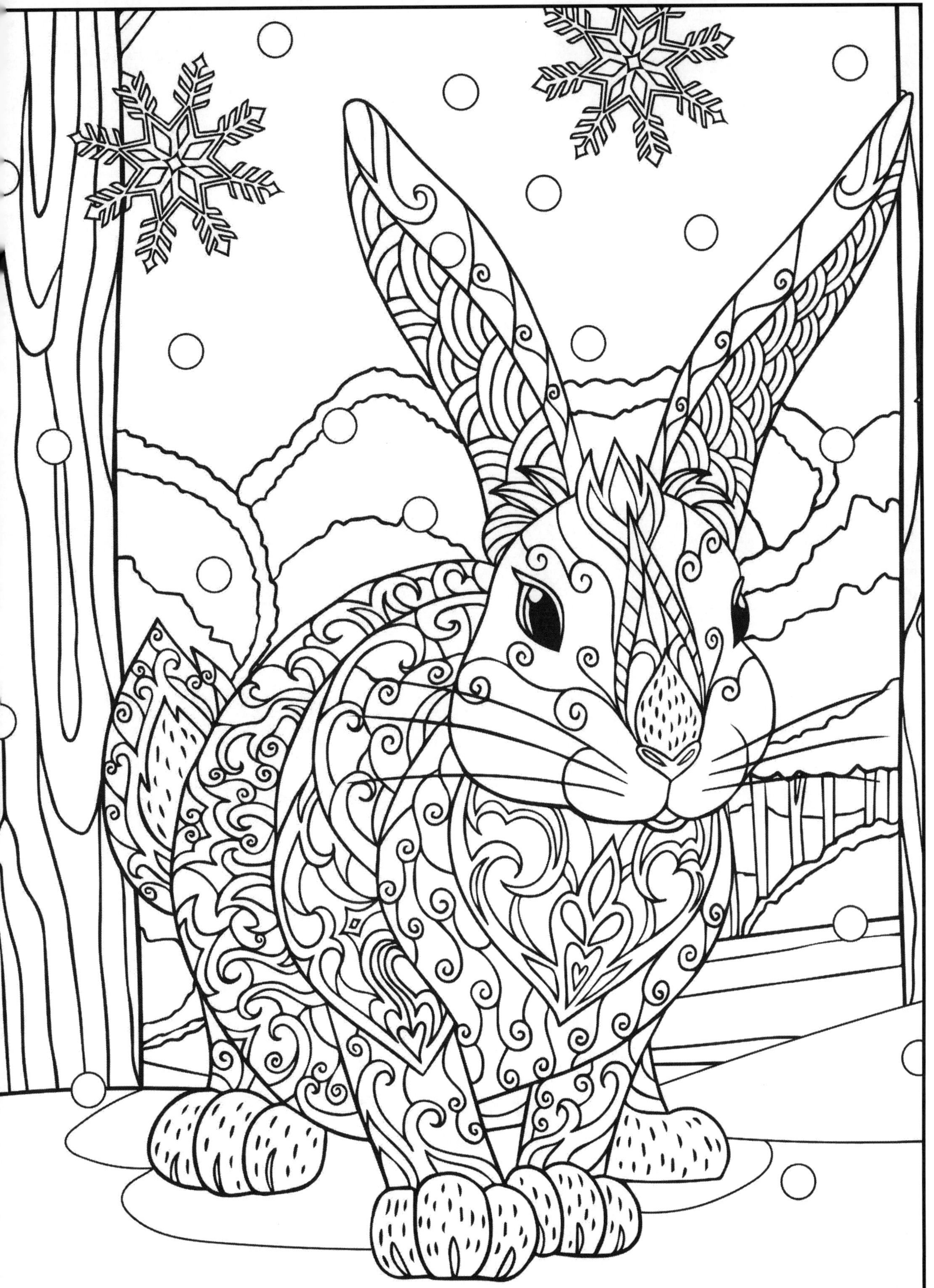

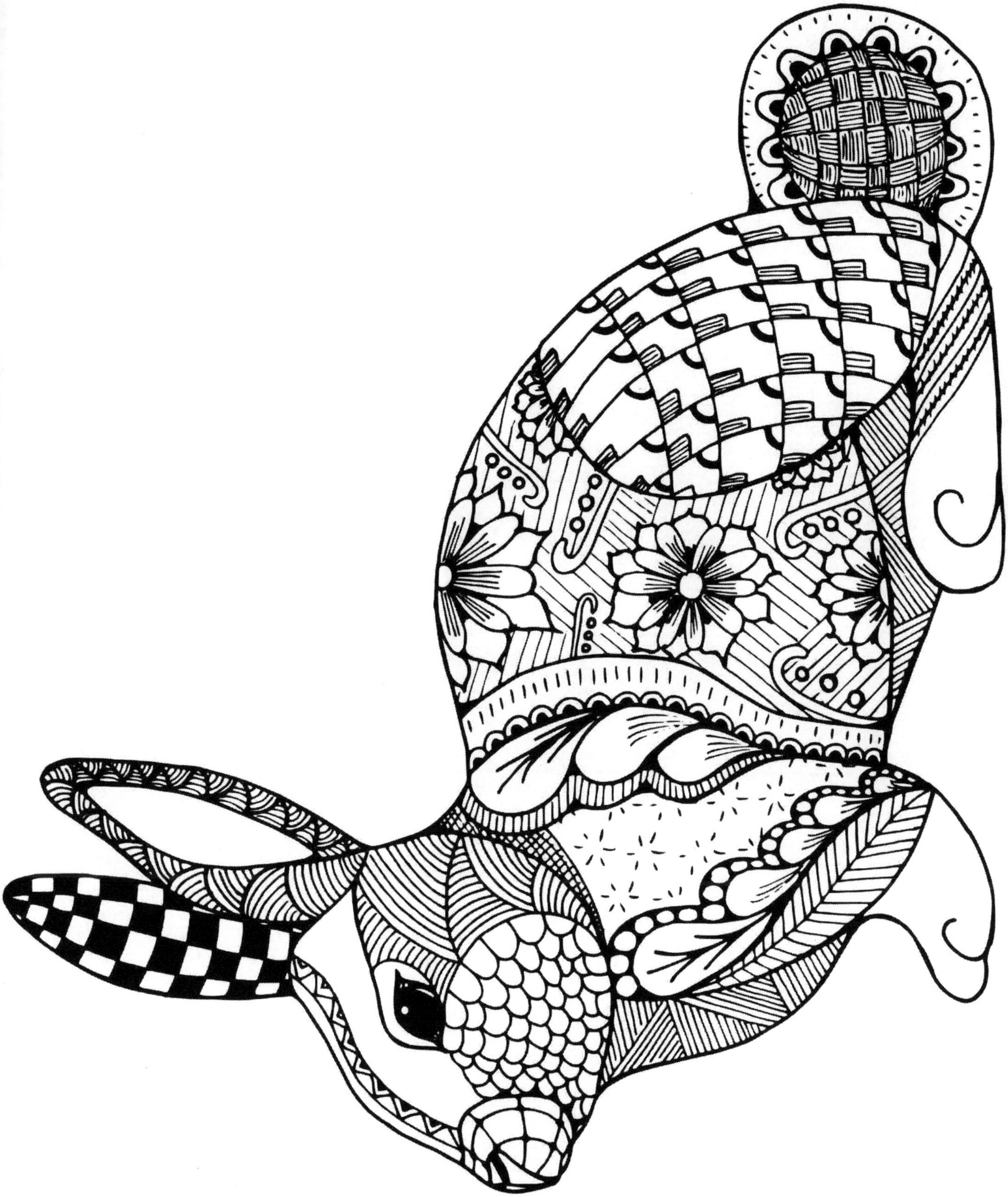

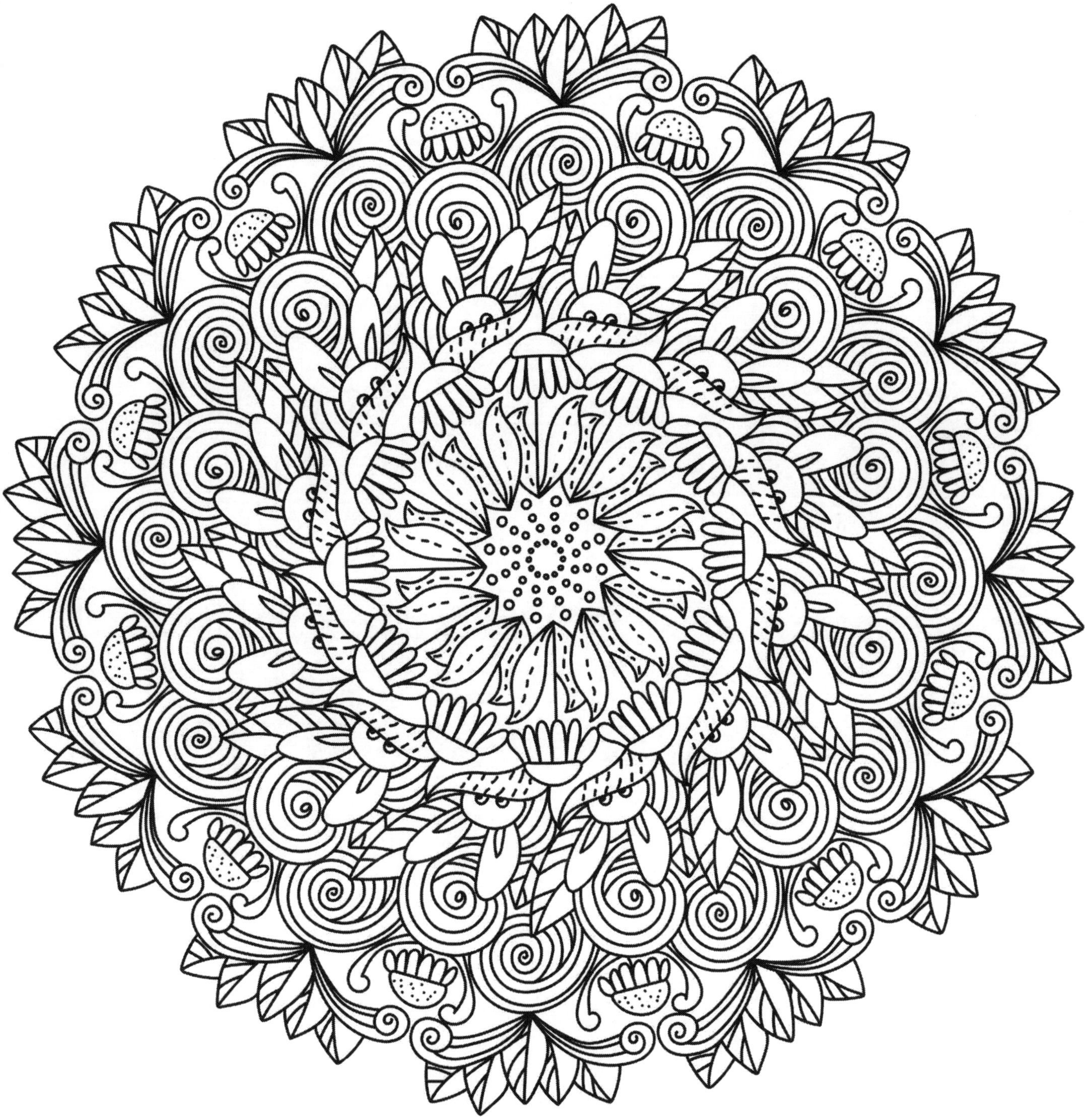

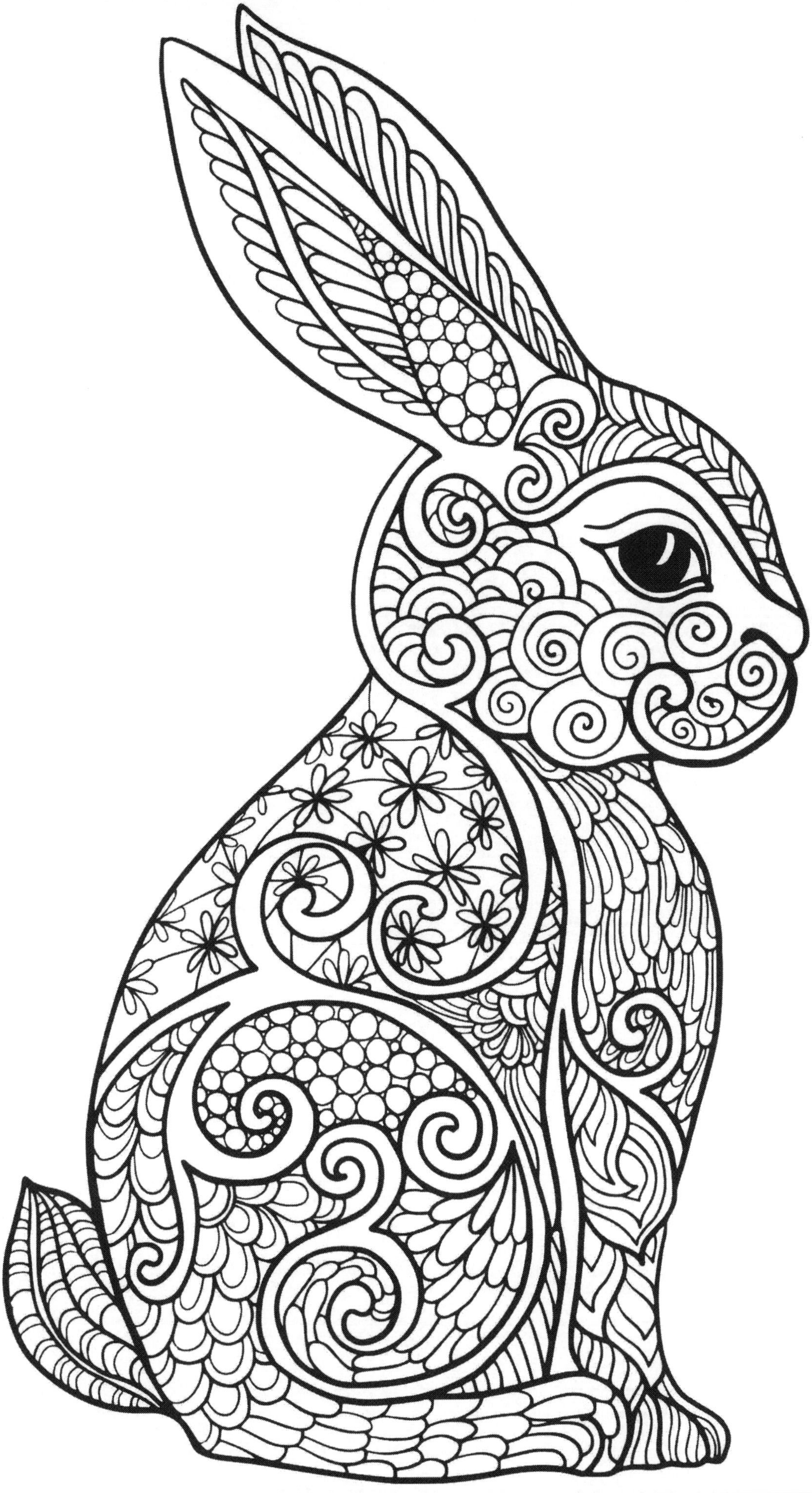

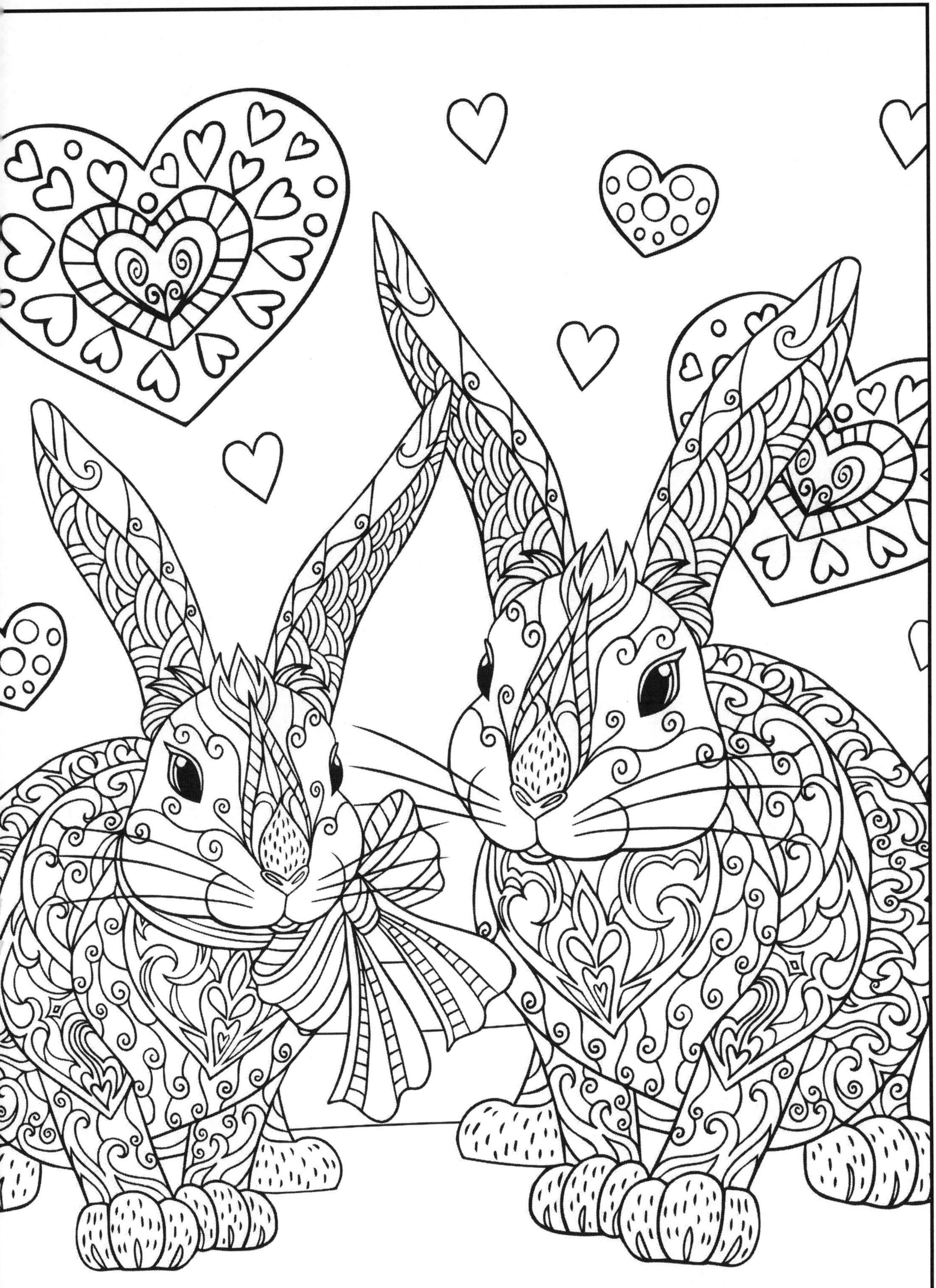

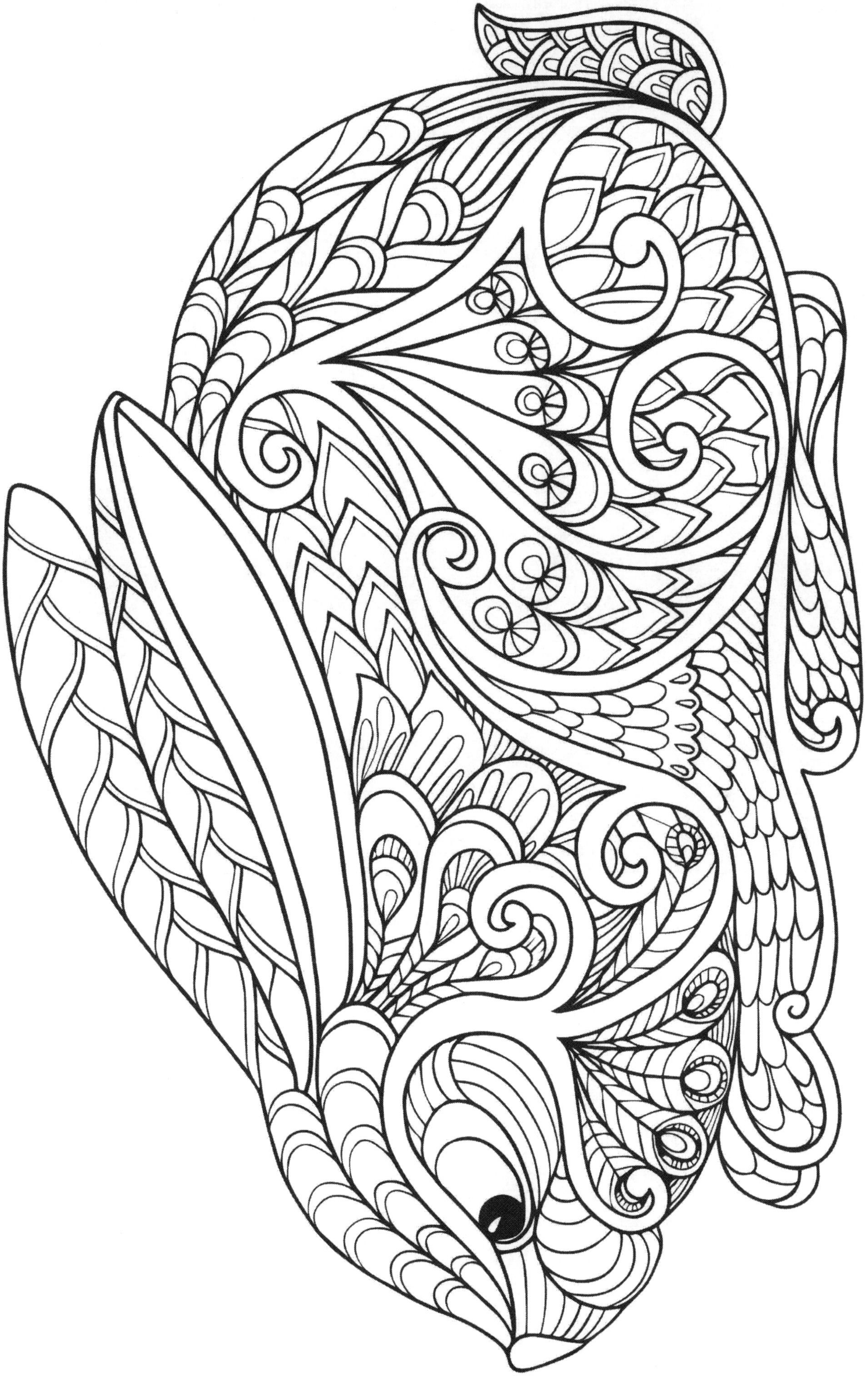

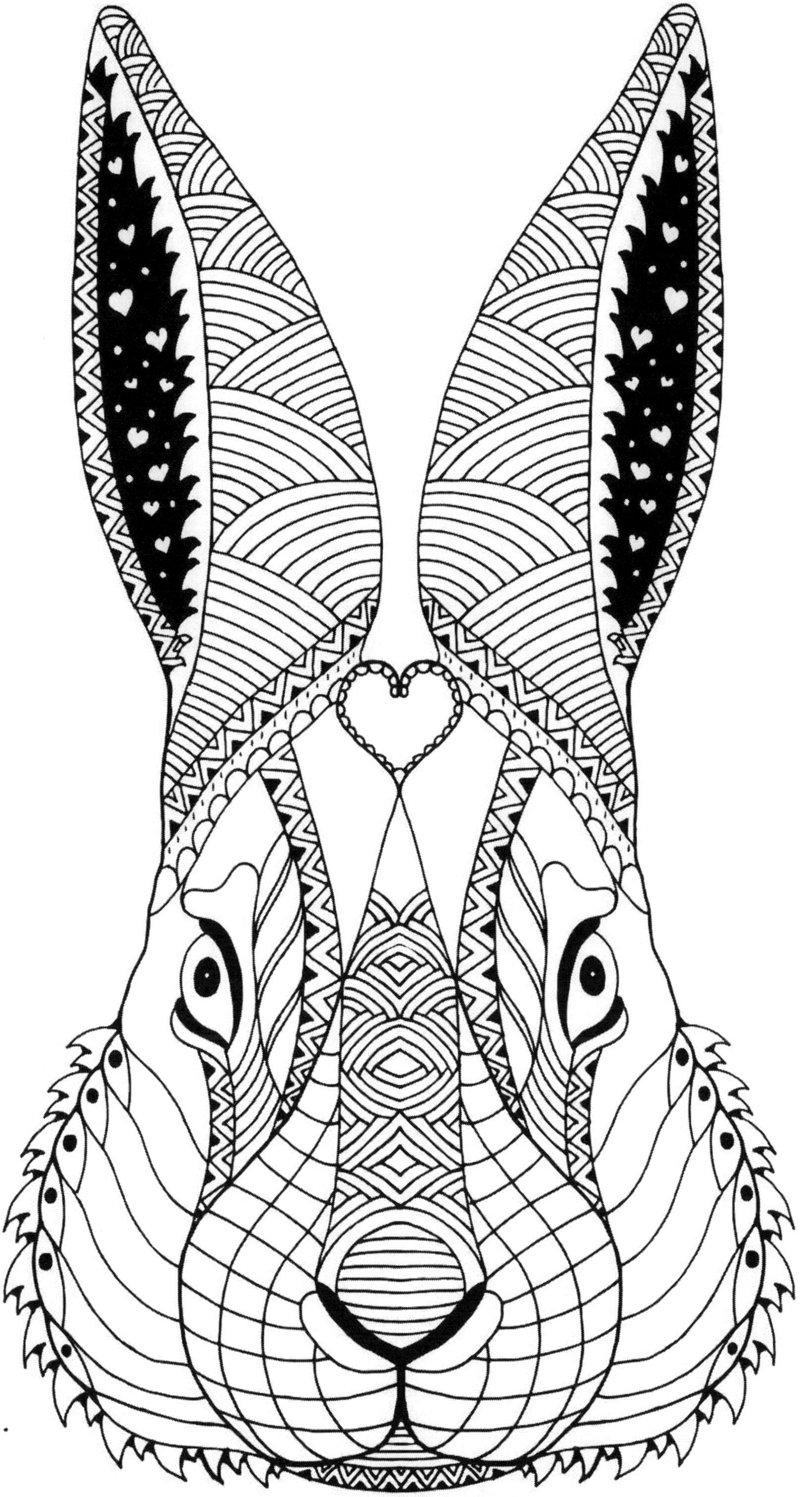

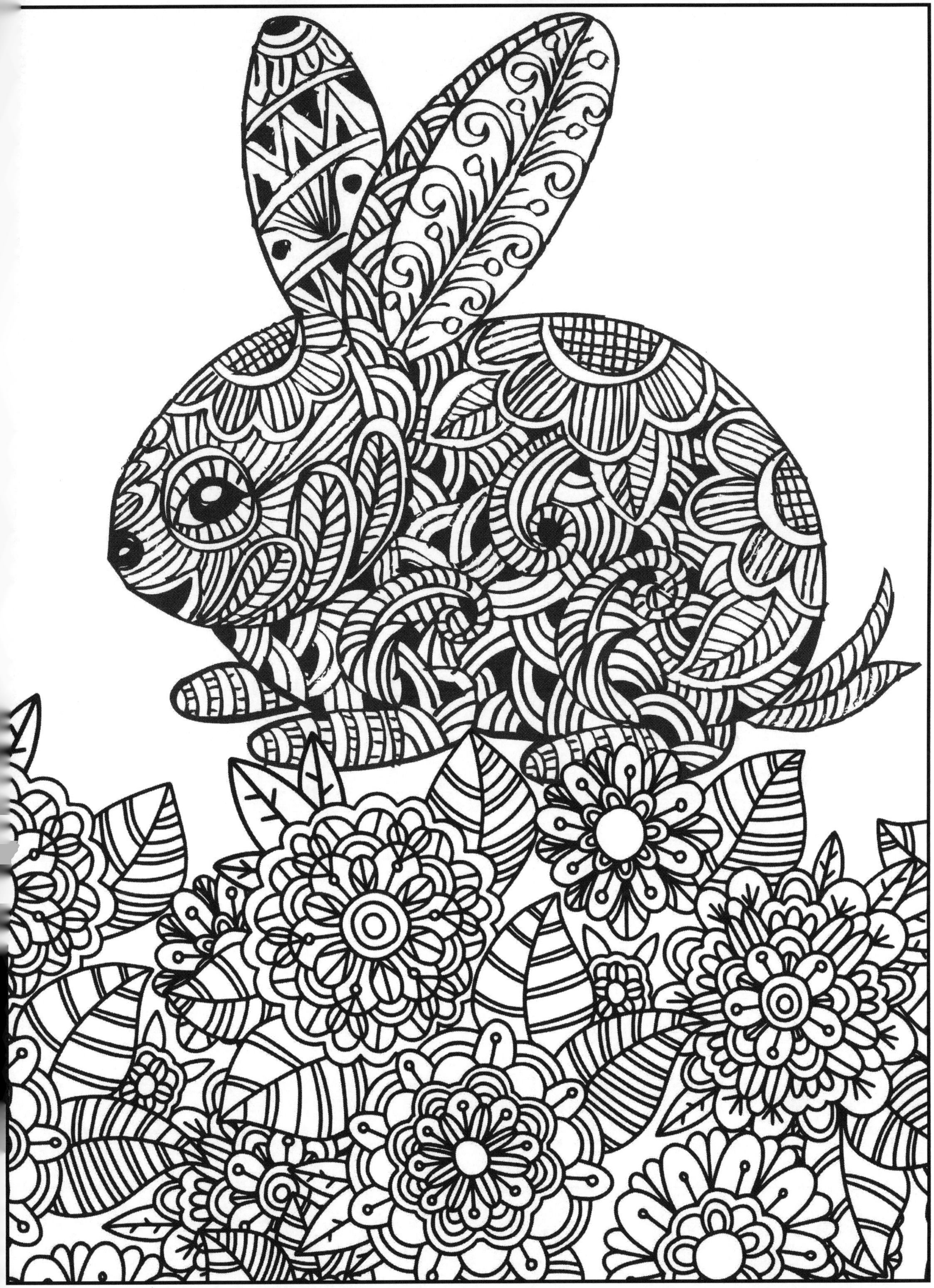

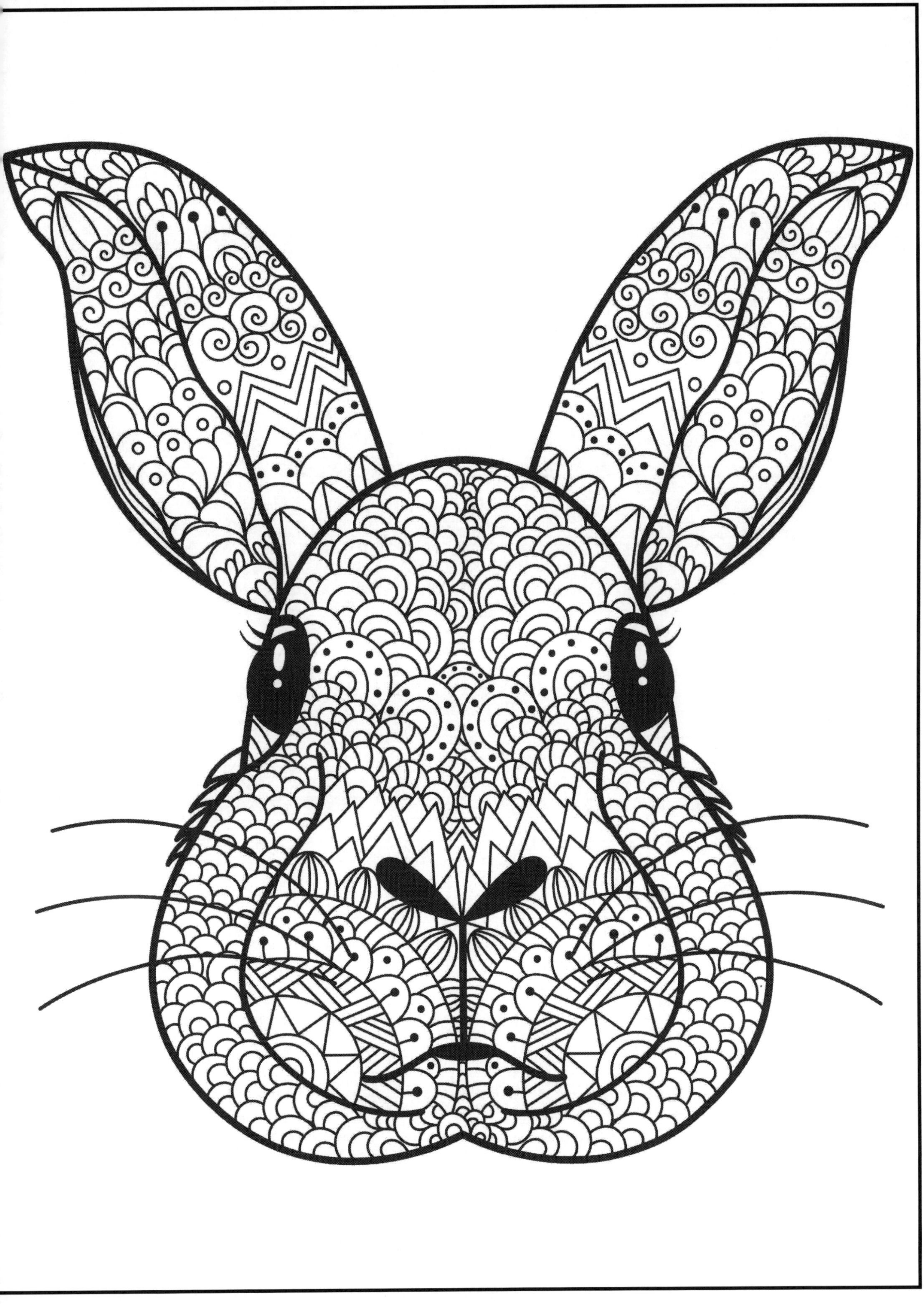

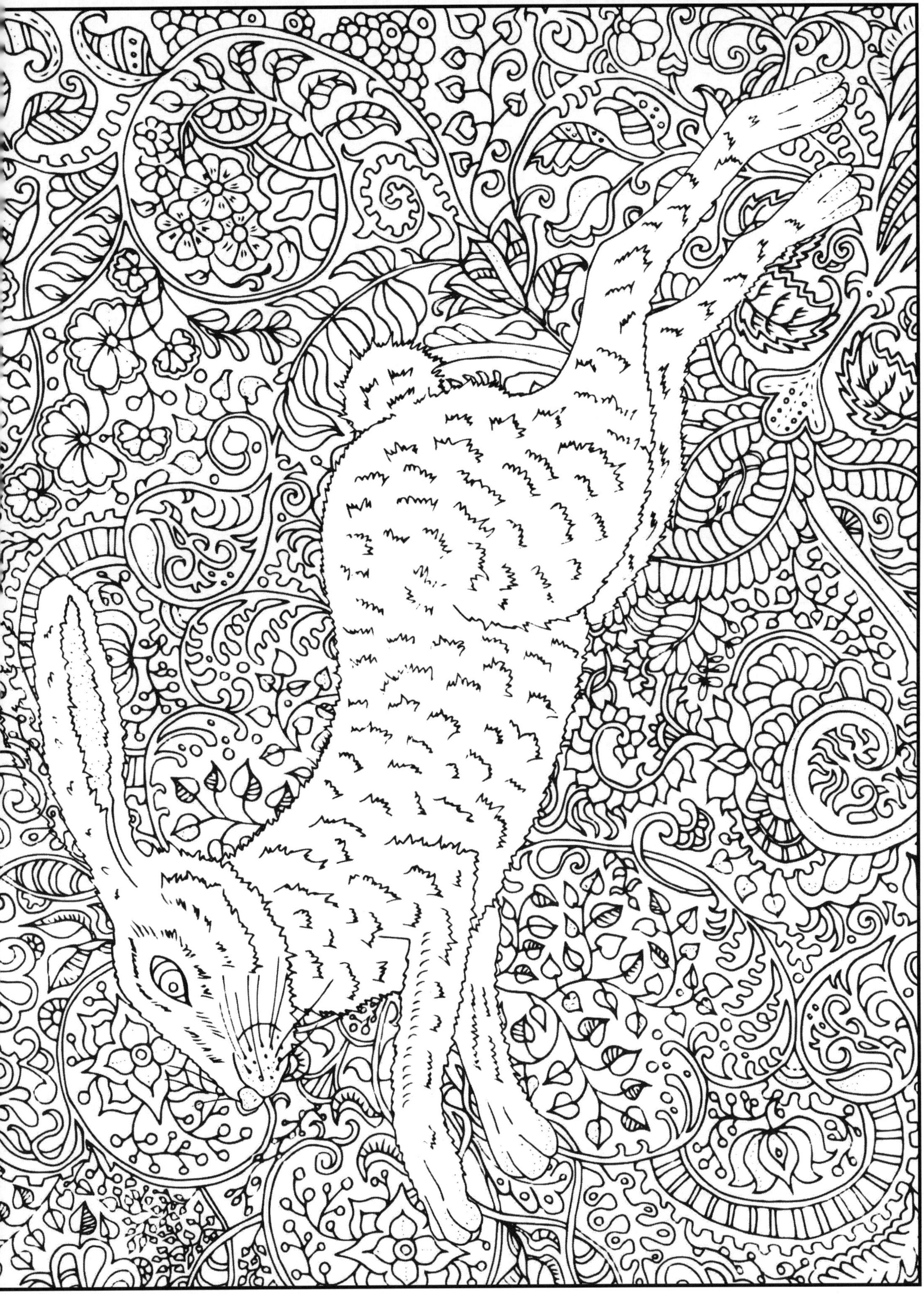

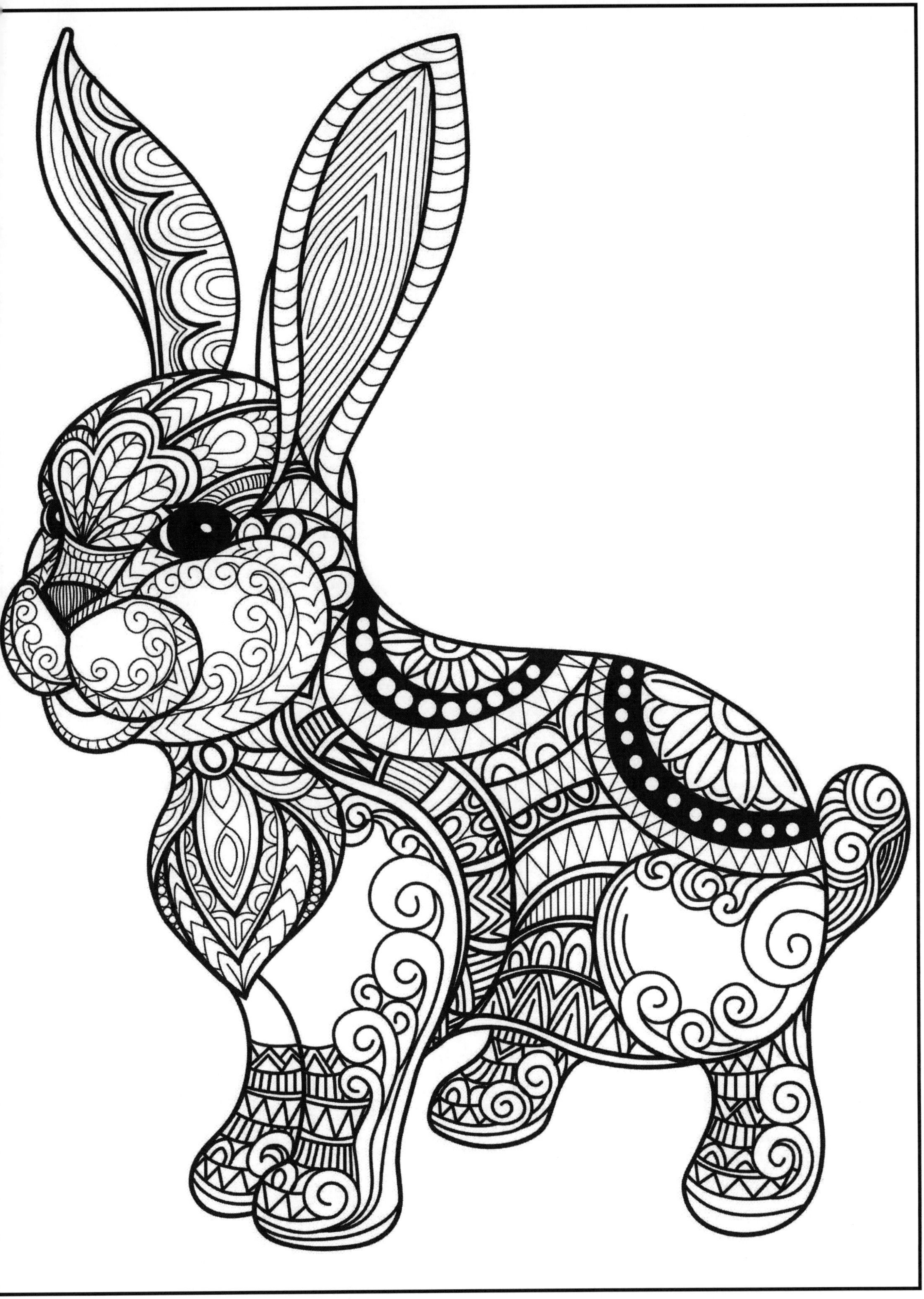

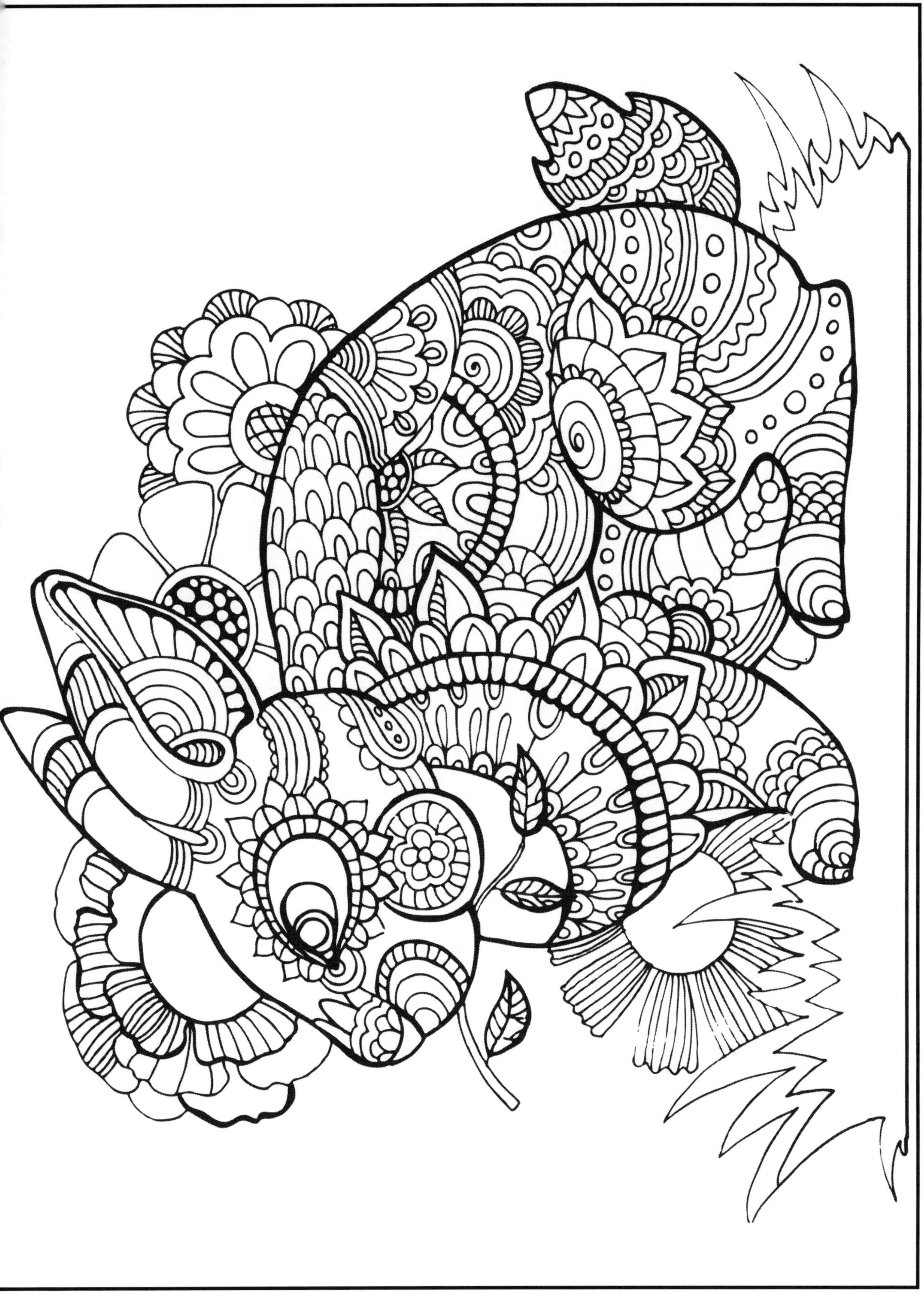

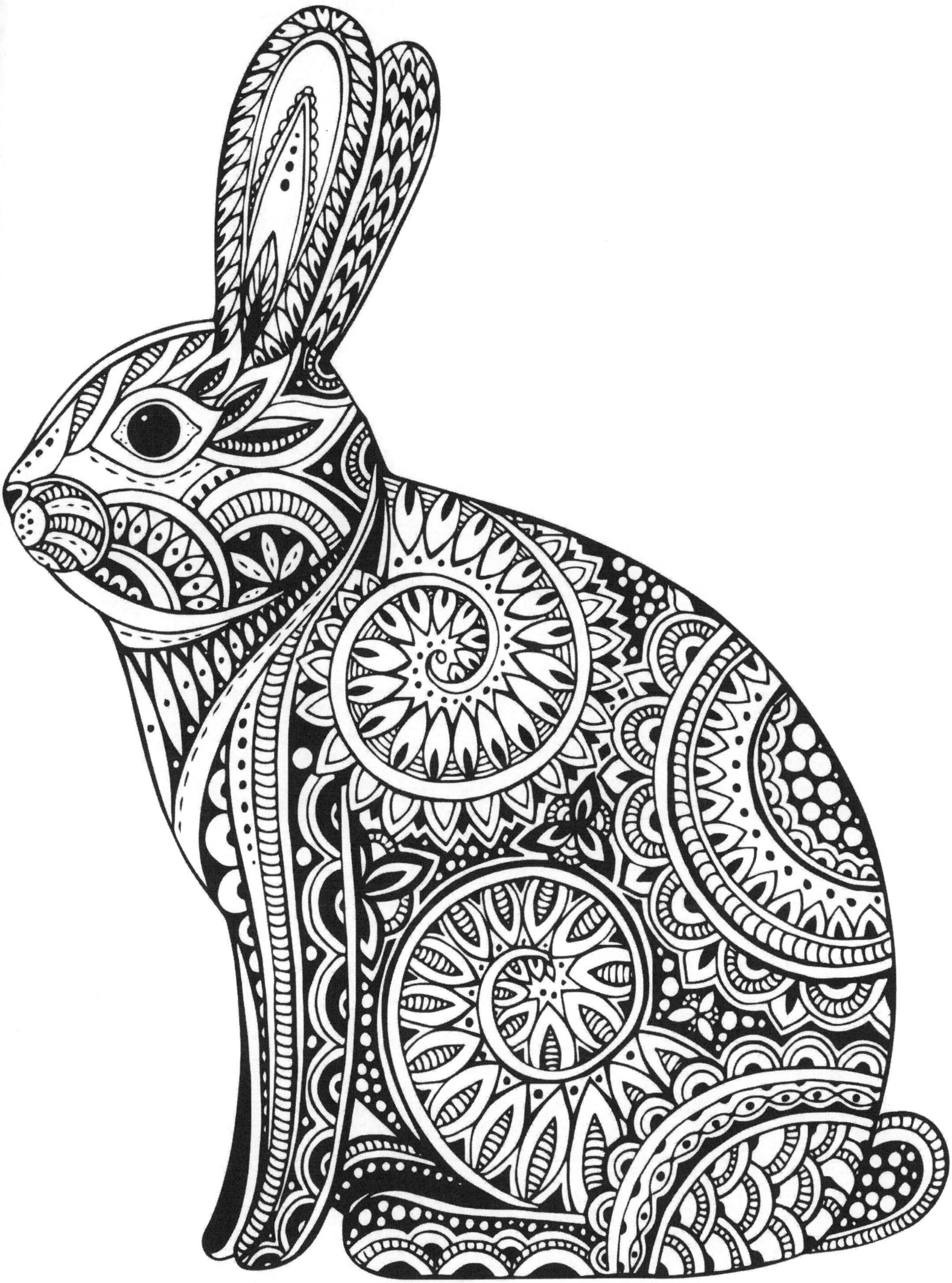

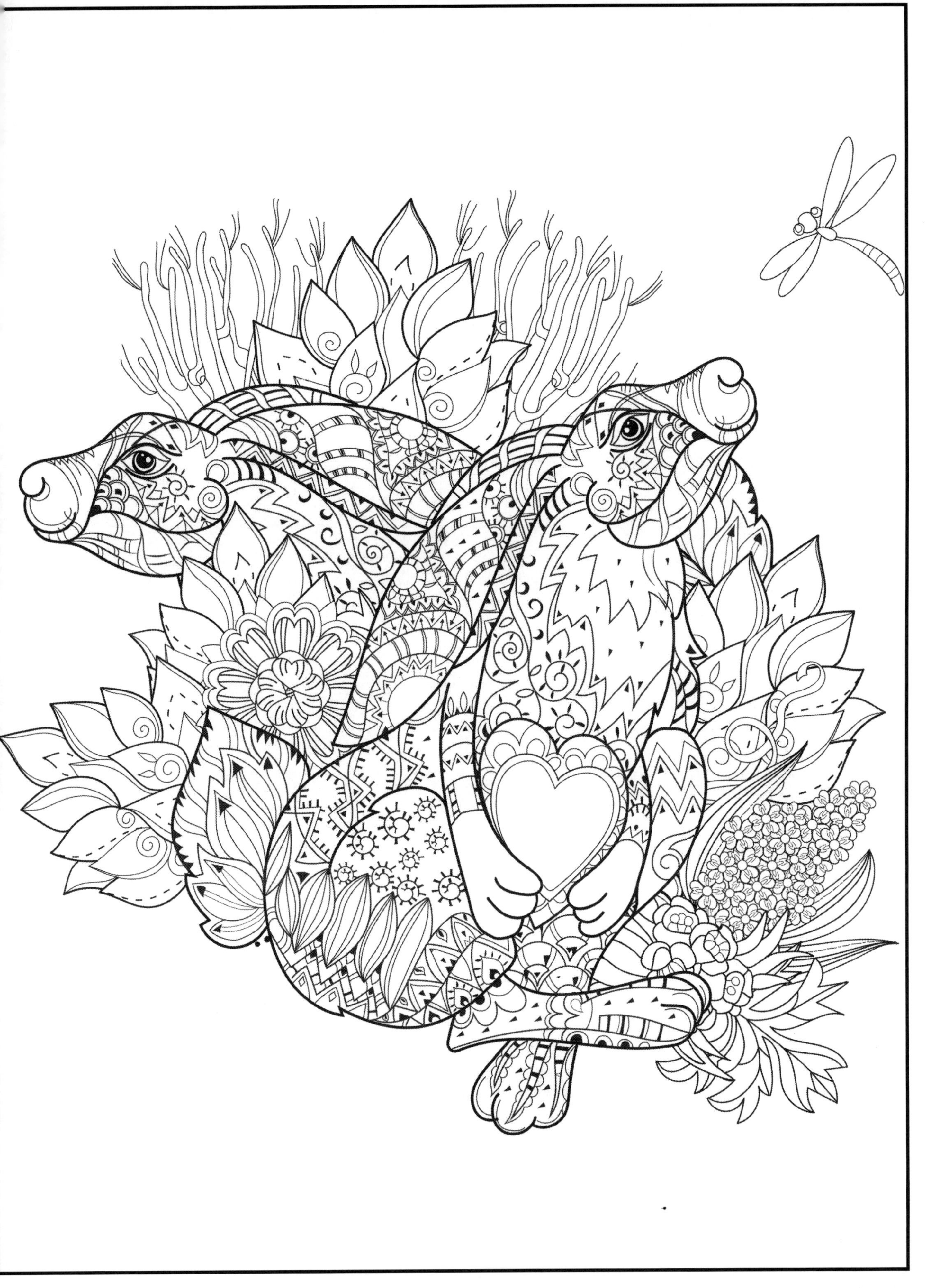

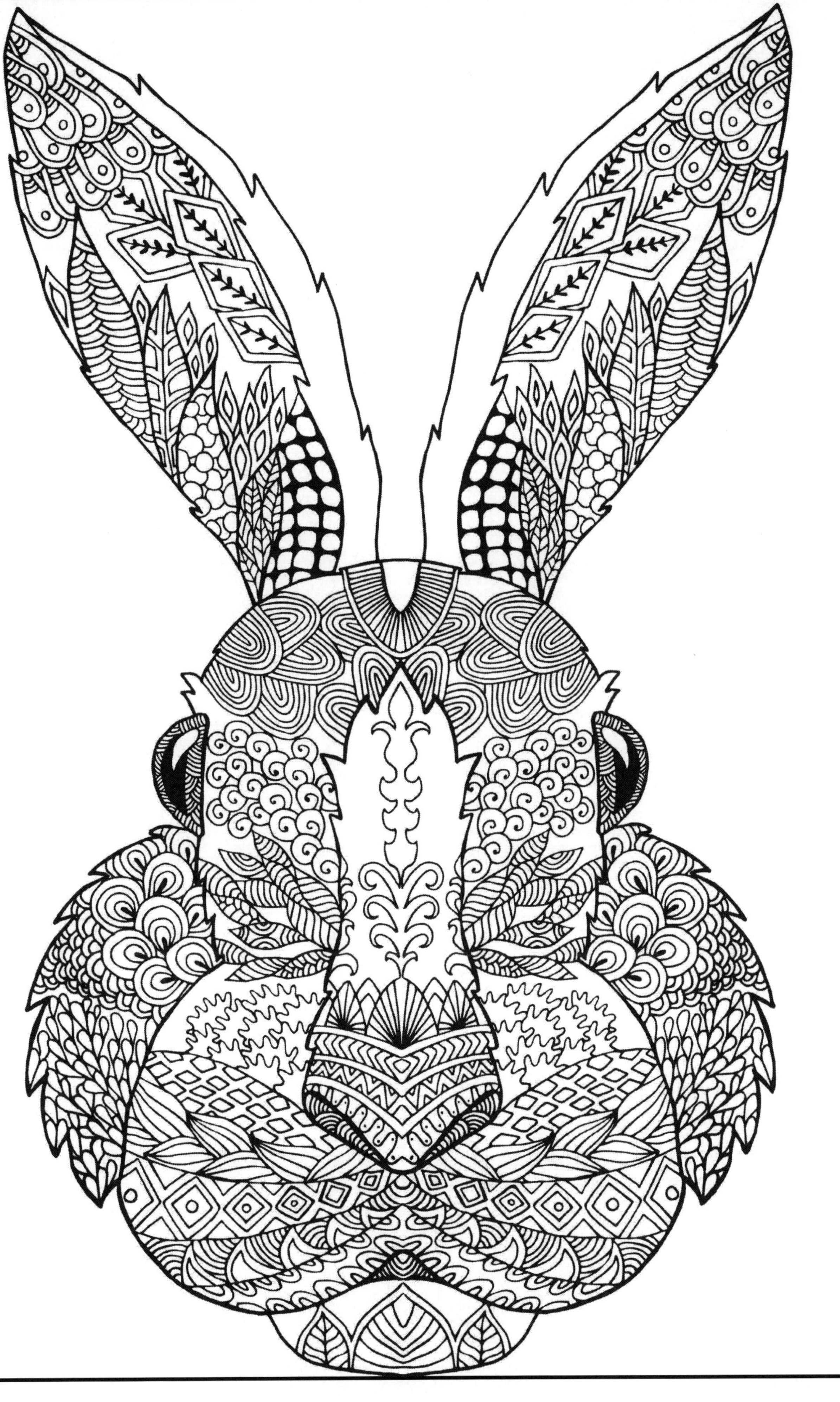

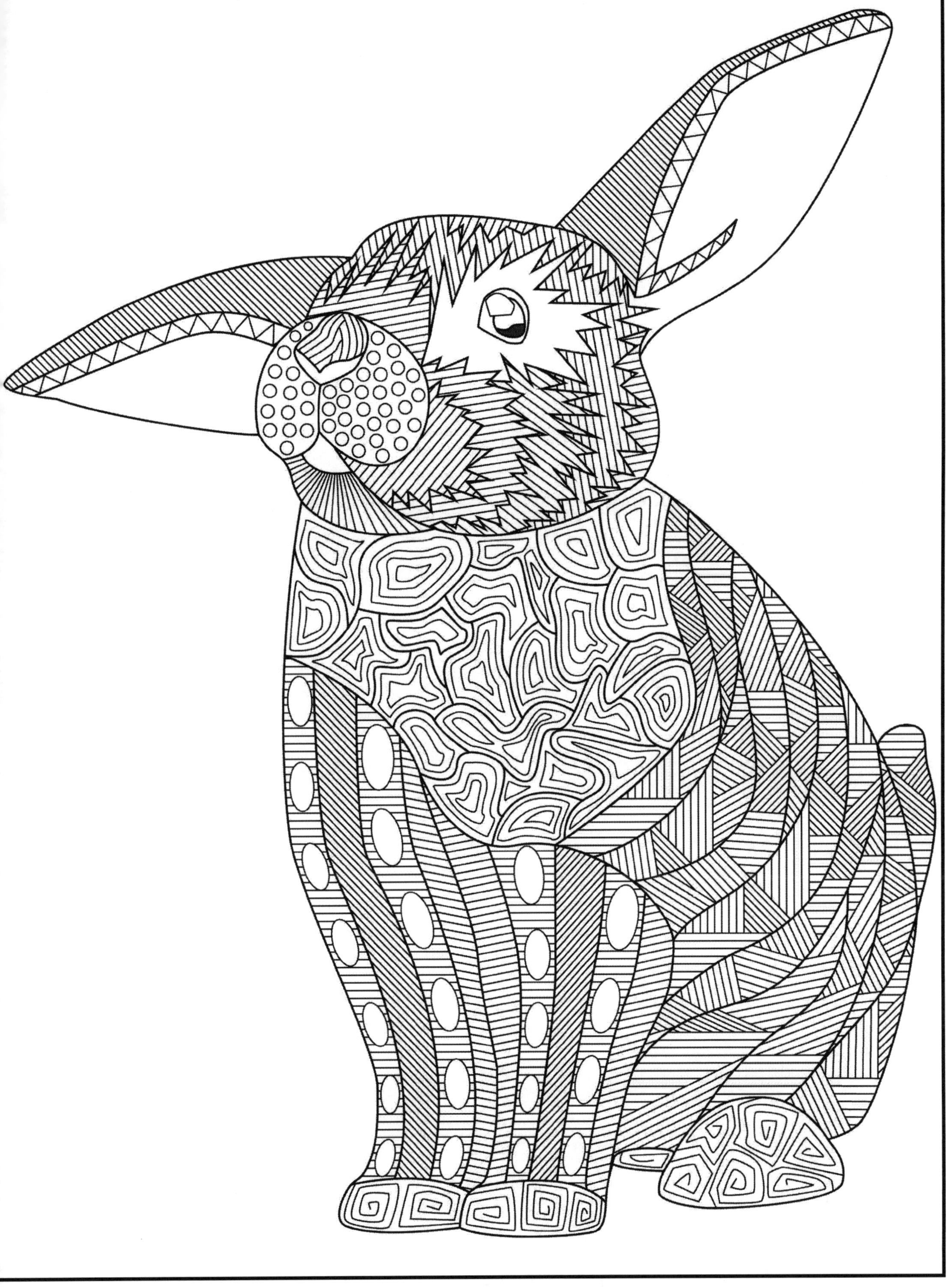

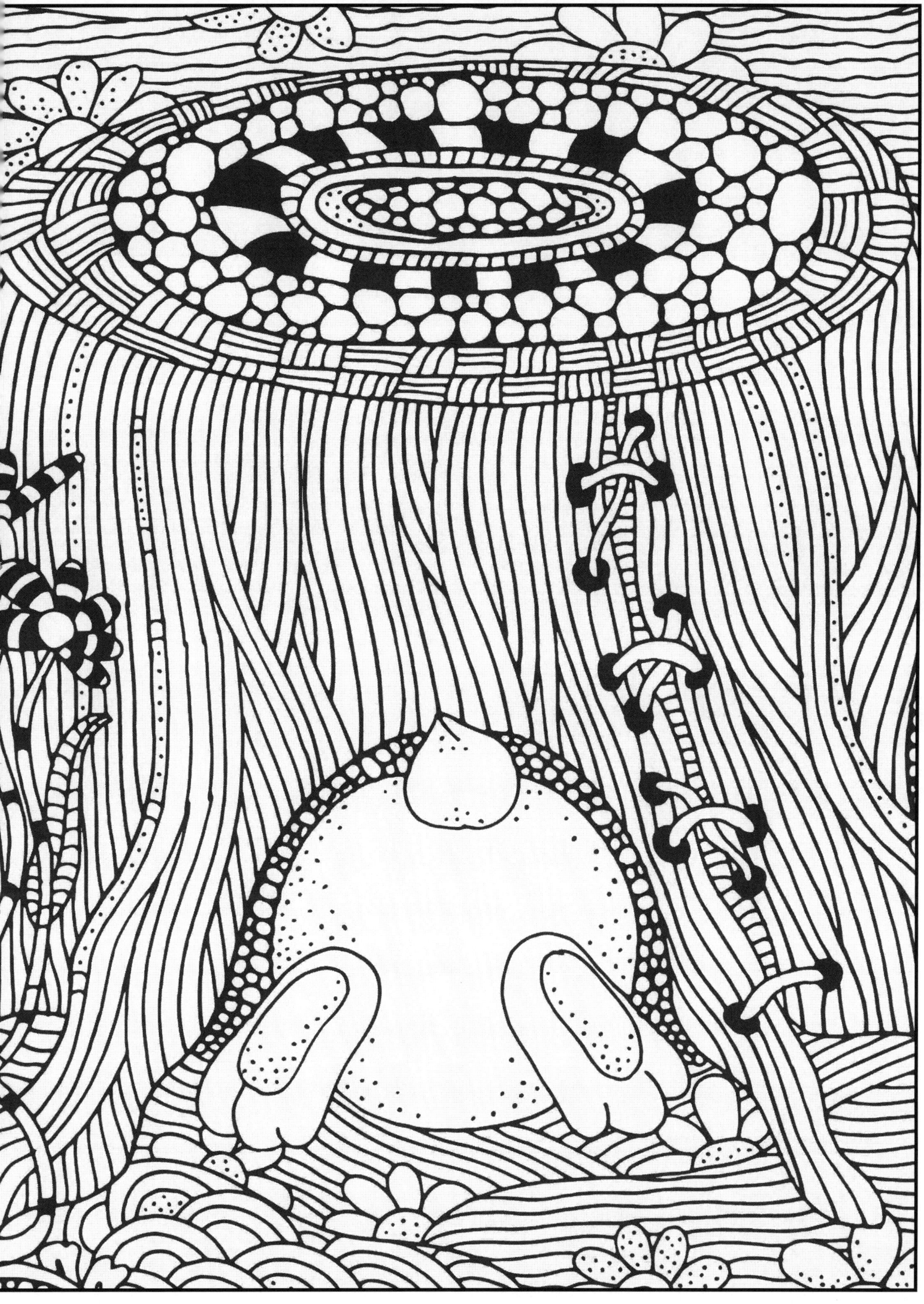

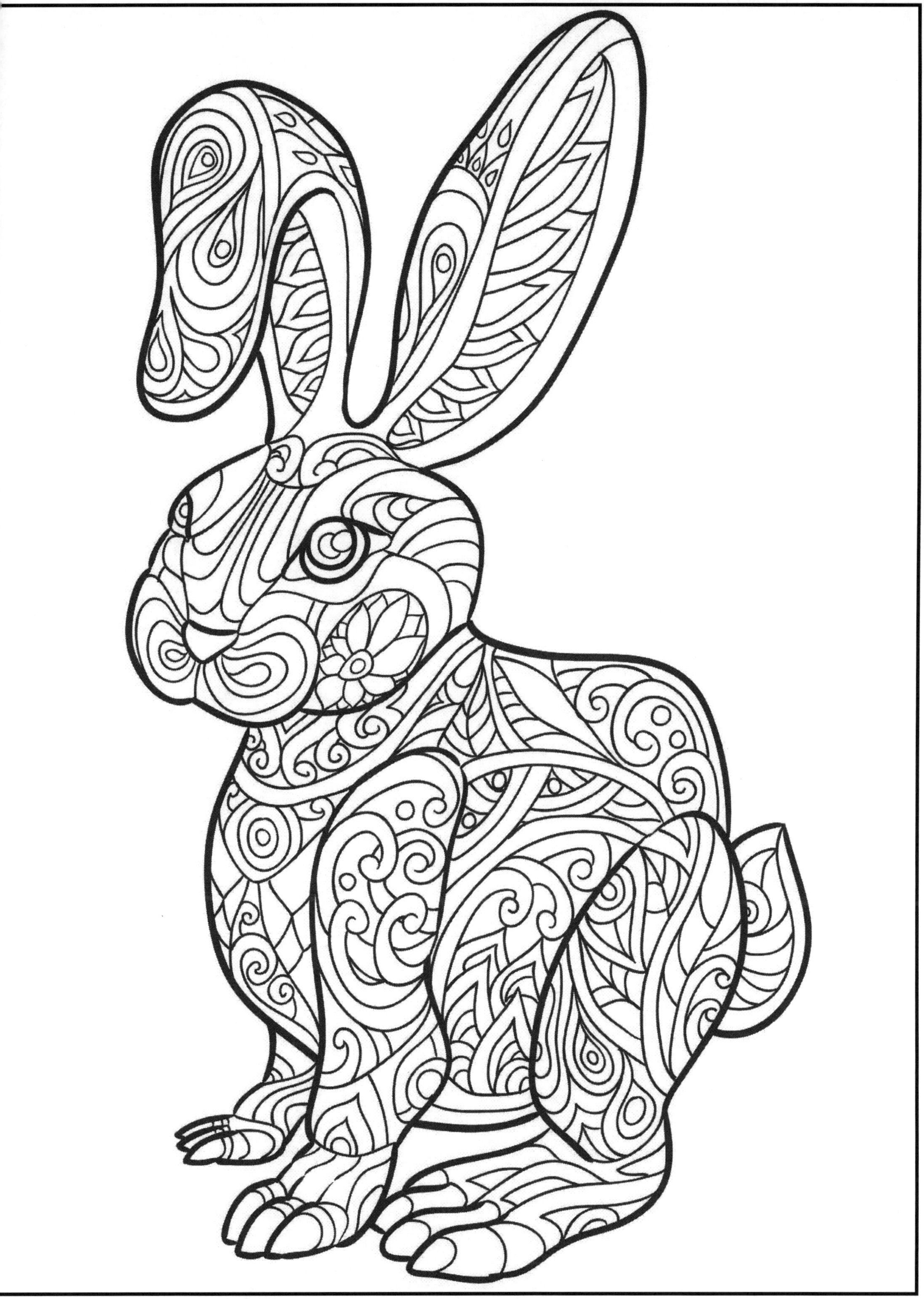

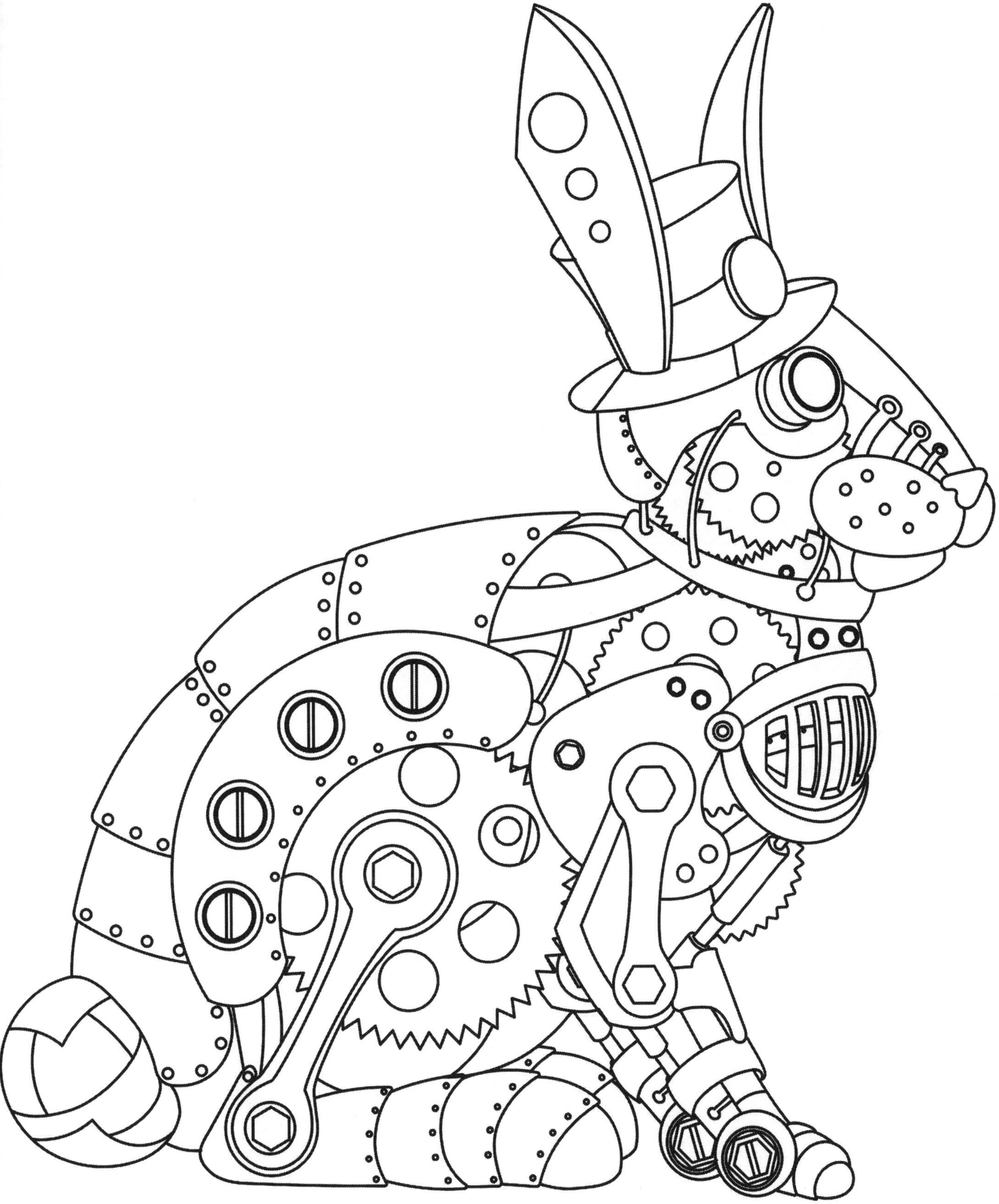

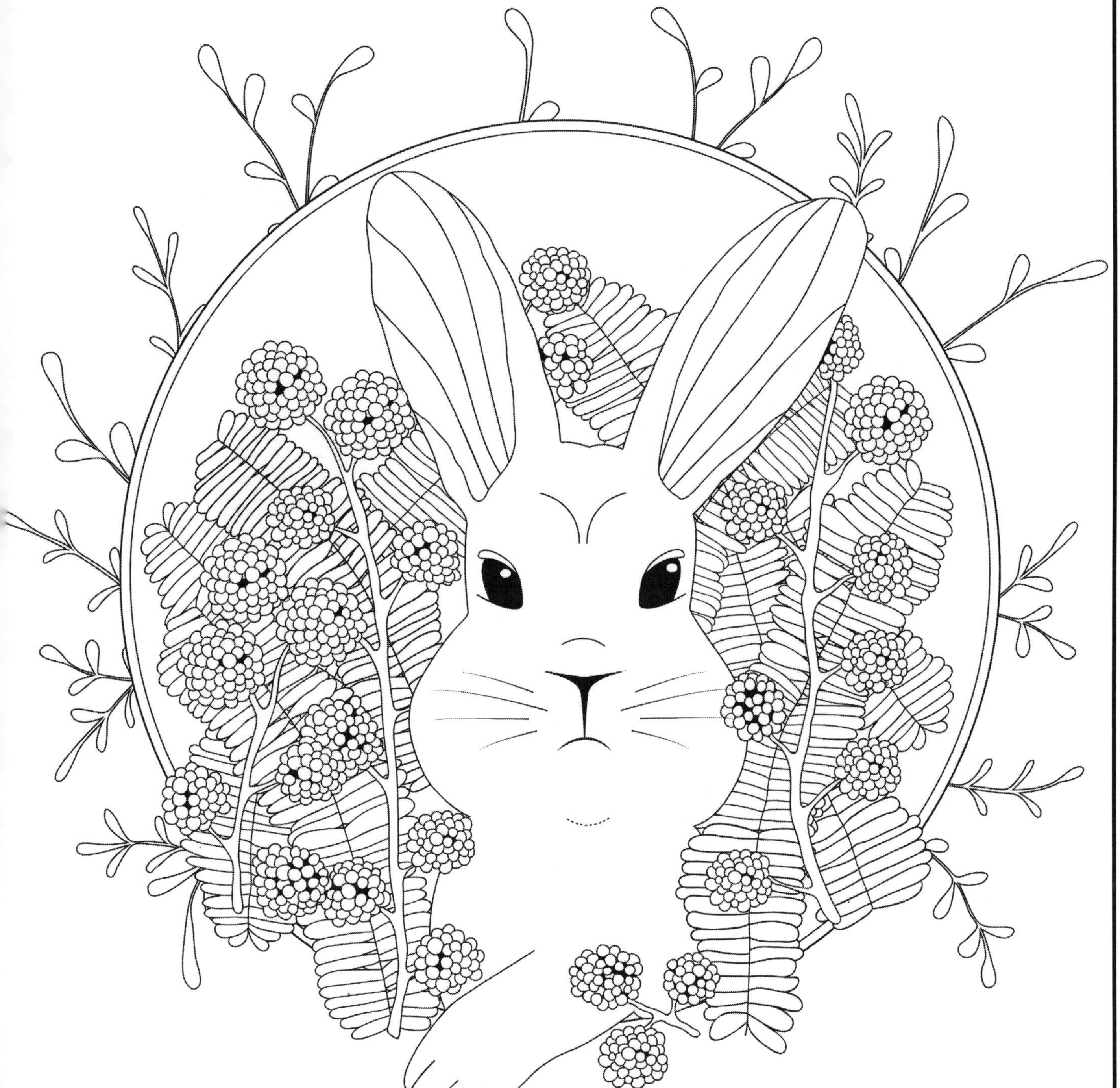

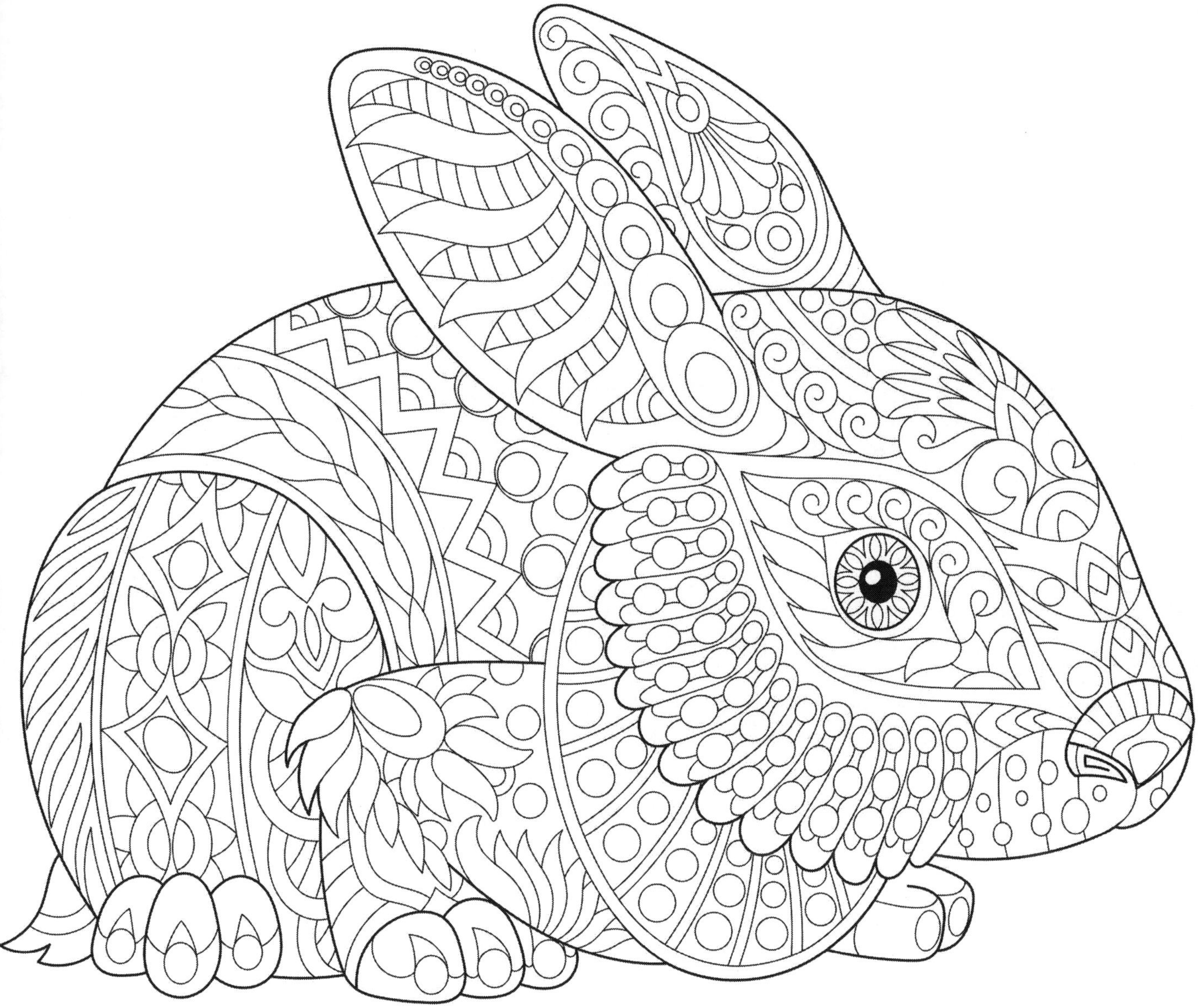

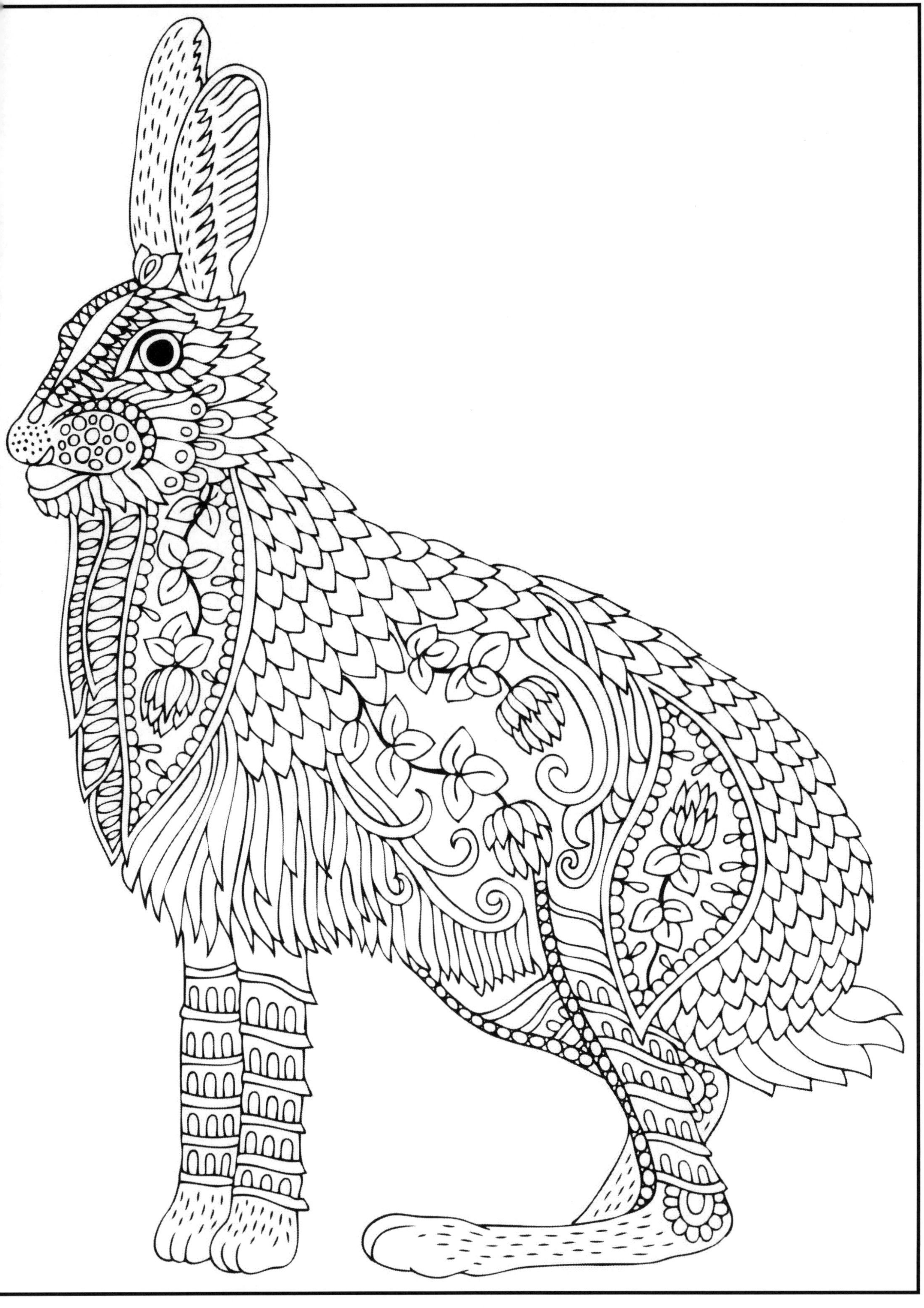

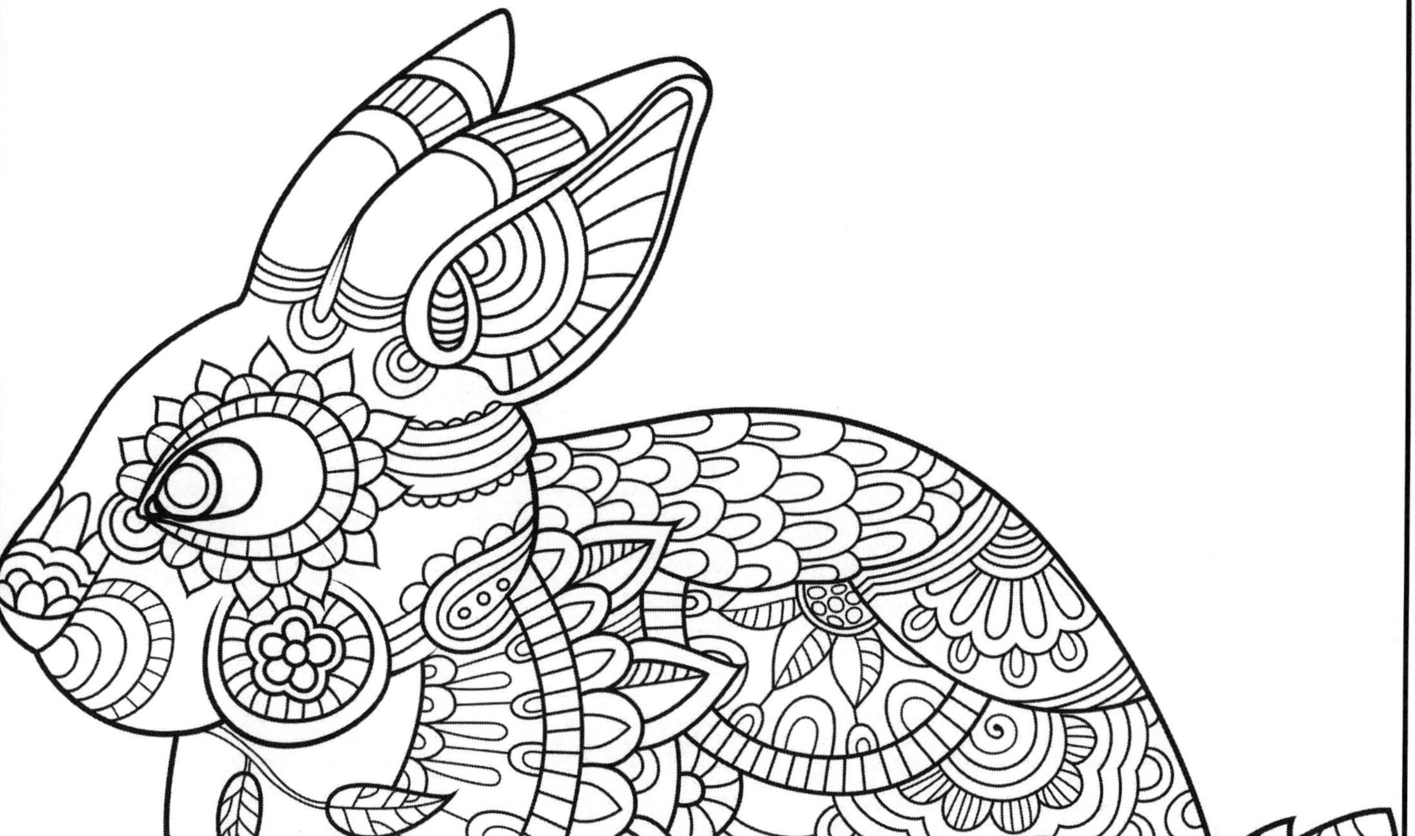

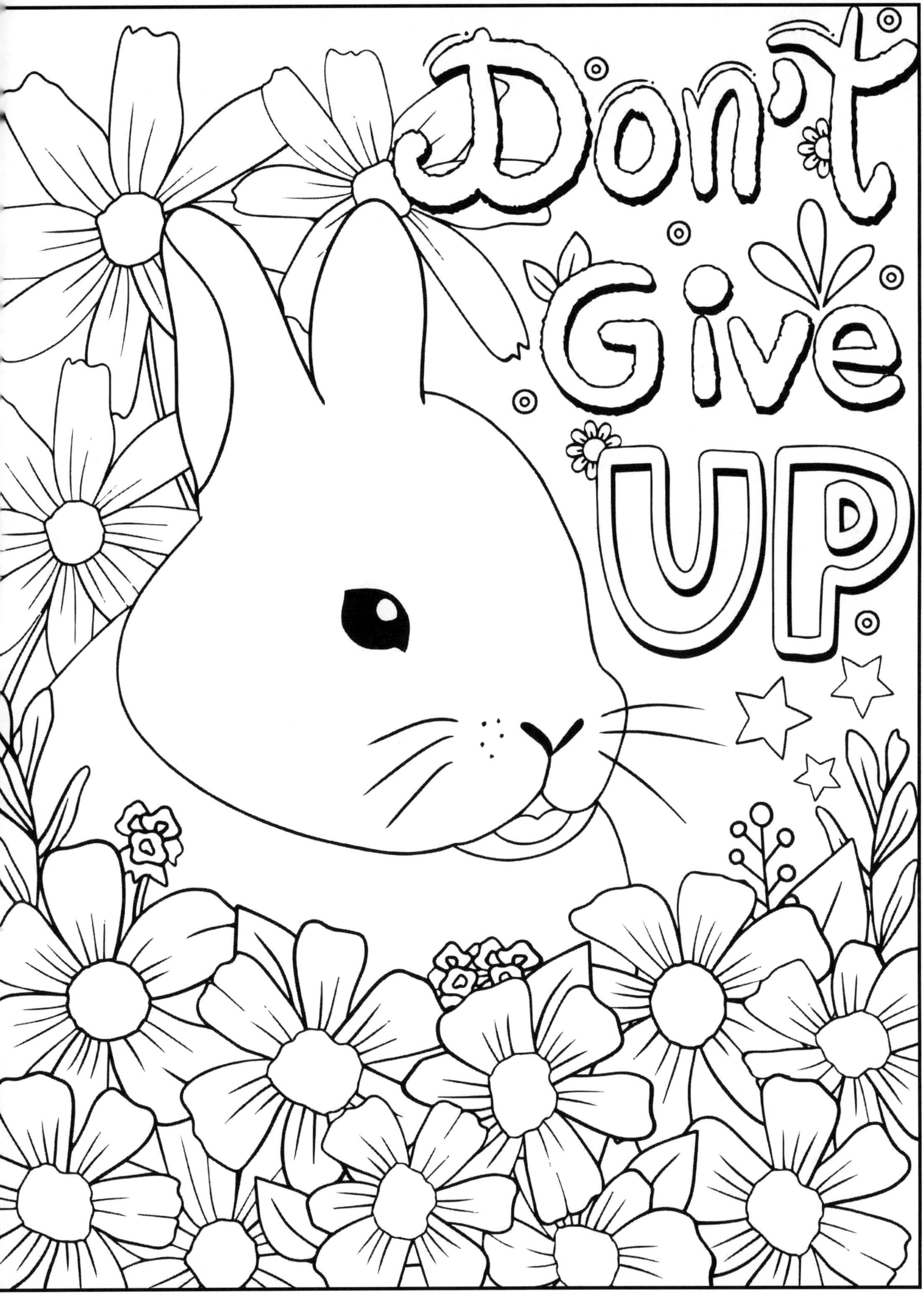
Don't Give UP

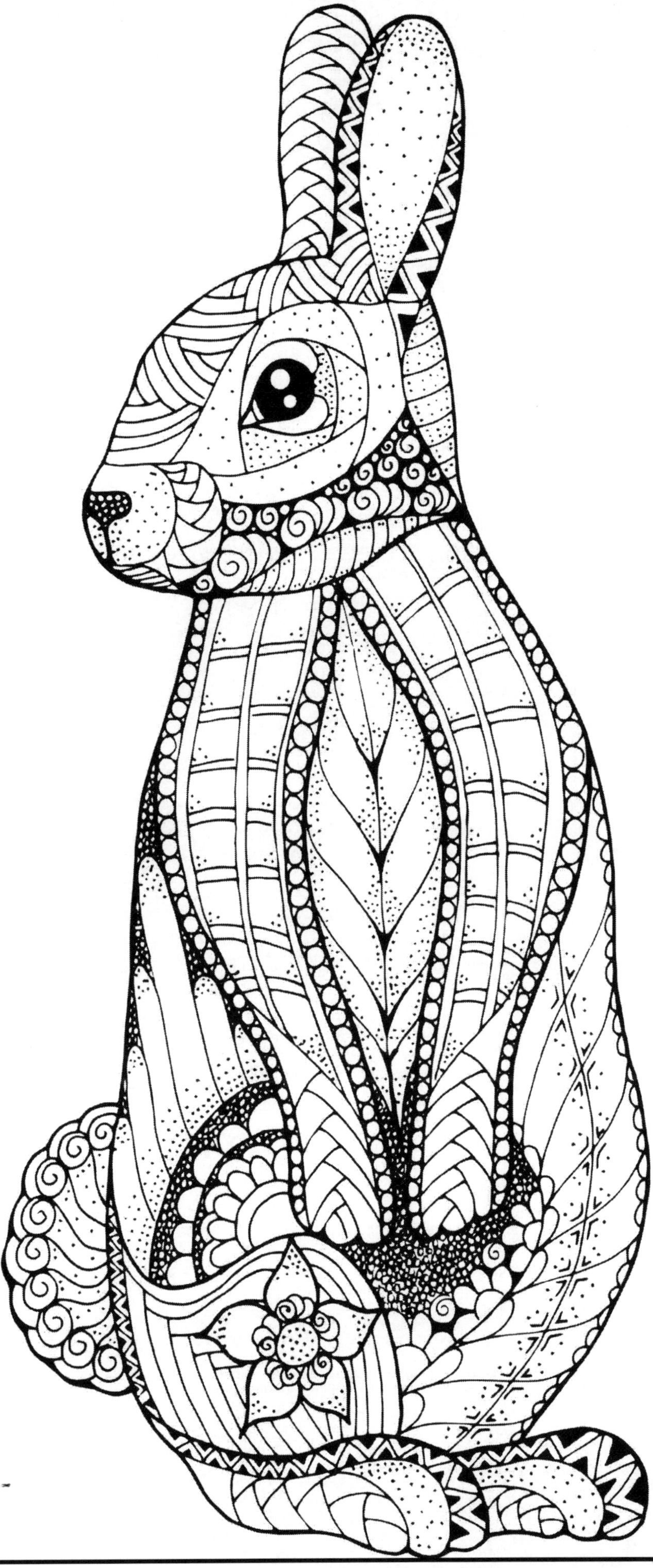

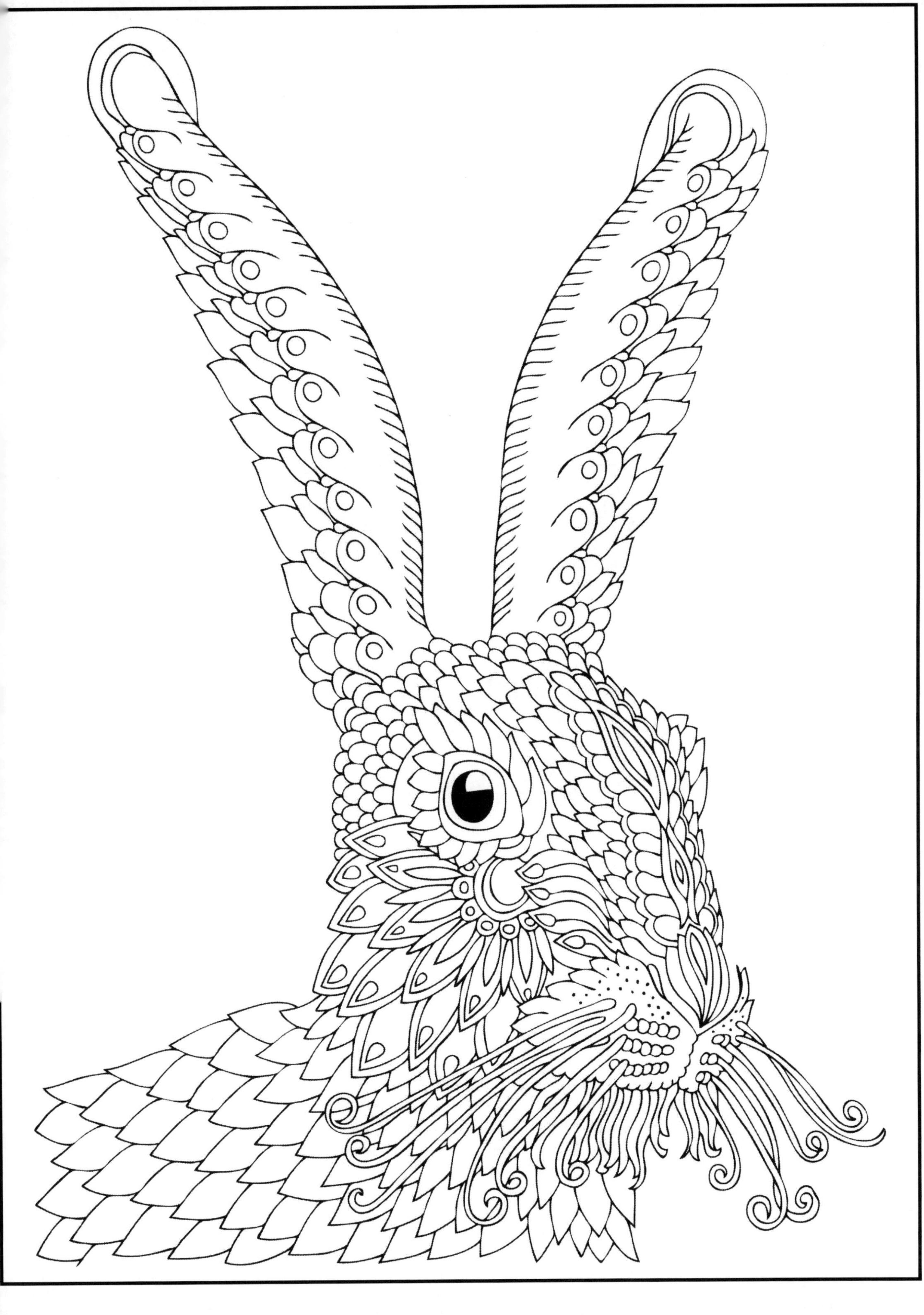

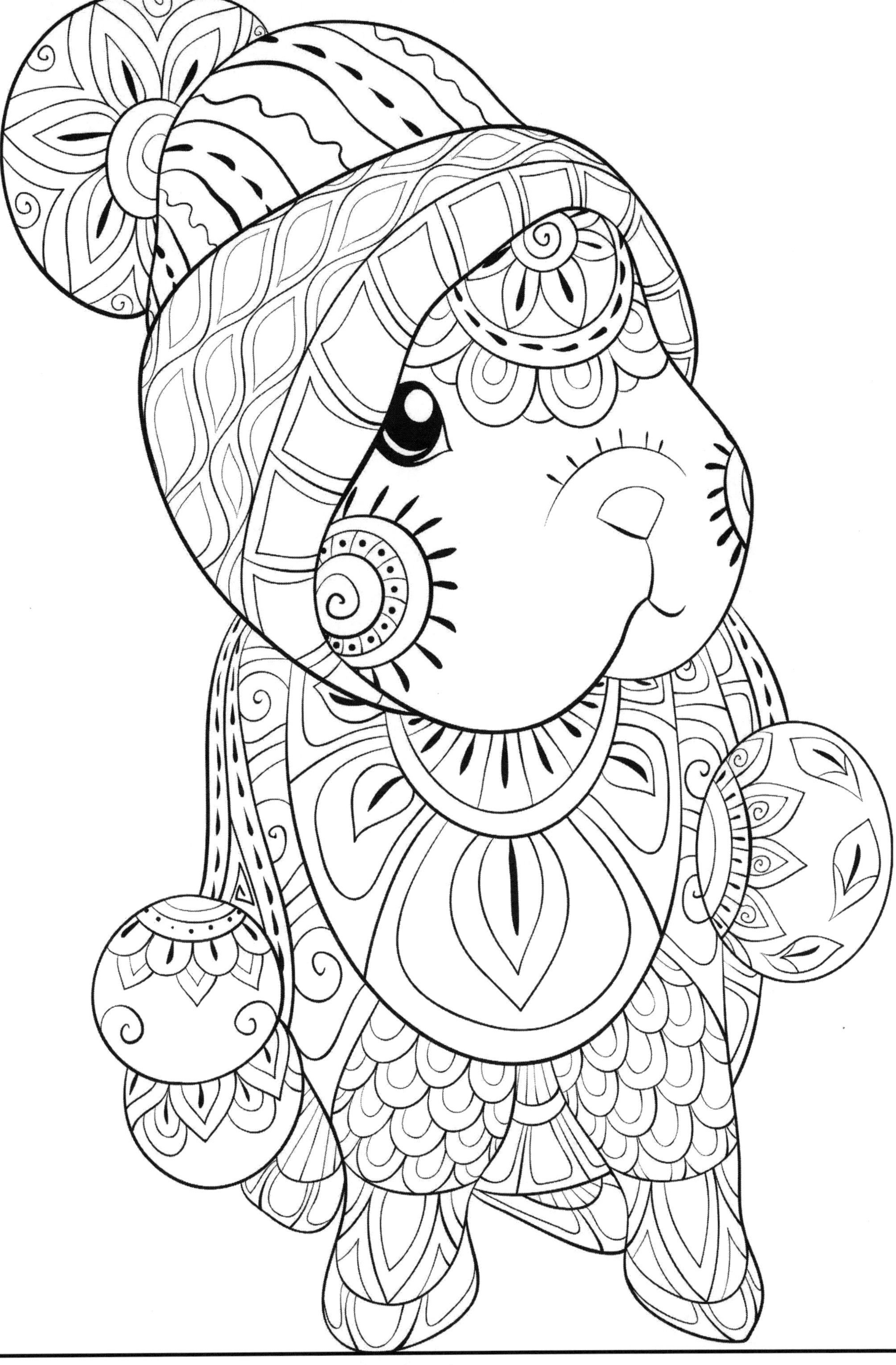

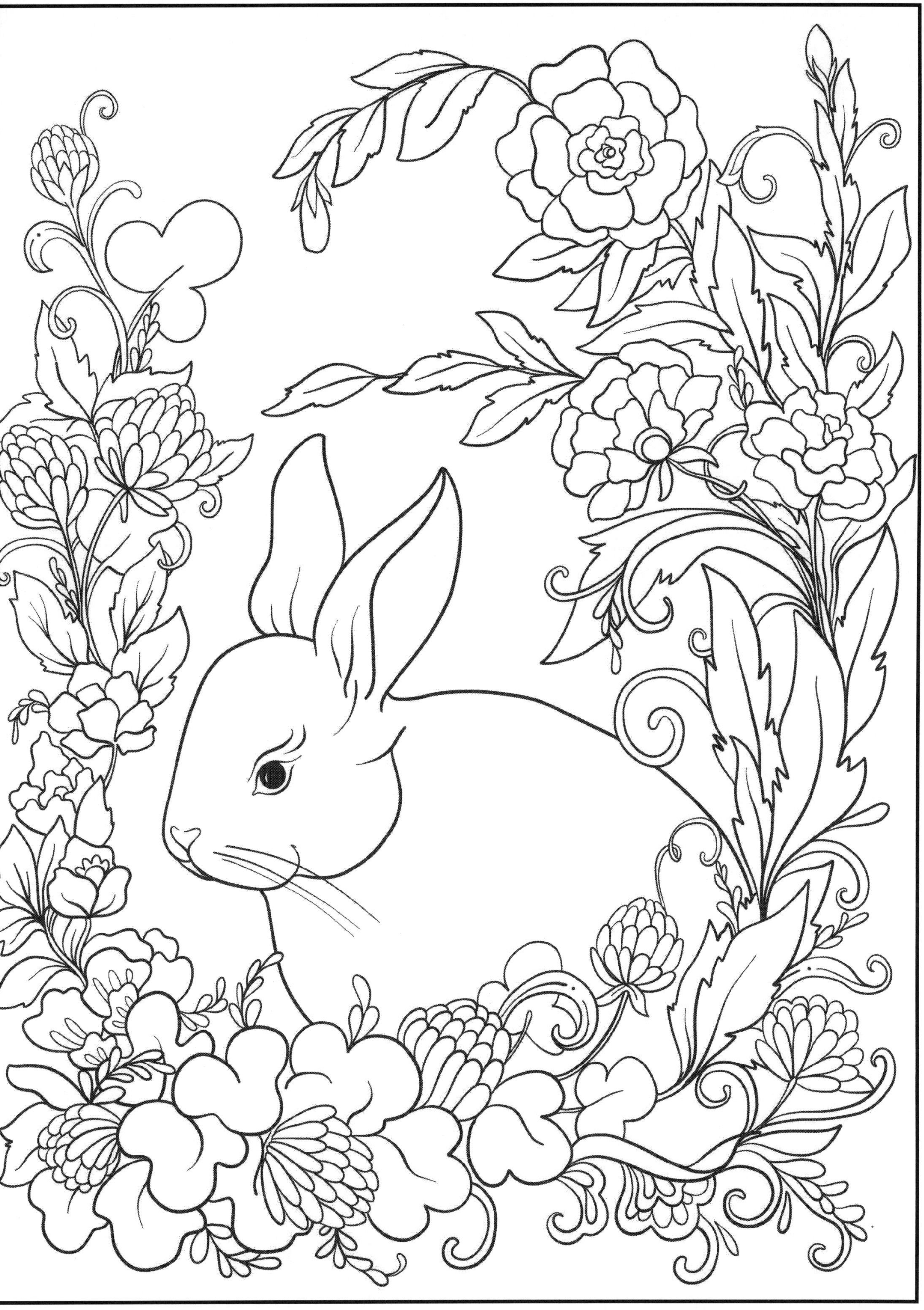

Made in United States
Orlando, FL
10 December 2022

26060458R00059